PROJECT STEM

SCIENCE • TECHNOLOGY • ENGINEERING • MATHEMATICS

Designing Space Vehicles

Grades 6–8

Glenview, Illinois • Boston, Massachusetts • Chandler, Arizona • Upper Saddle River, New Jersey

Project STEM

Introduction to STEM

Building Space Vehicles

Appendices

Review the Safety Symbols pages before beginning each topic.

The Engineering Design Process

Engineers are people who use scientific and technological knowledge to solve practical problems. To design new products, engineers usually follow the process described here, even though they may not follow these steps in the same order each time.

Identify a Need

Before engineers begin designing a new product, they must first identify the need they are trying to meet or the problem they want to solve. For example, suppose you are a member of a design team in a company that makes model cars. Your team has identified a need: a model car that is inexpensive and easy to assemble.

Research the Problem

Engineers often begin by gathering information that will help them with their new design. This research may include finding articles in books, in journals, or on the Internet. It may also involve talking to other engineers who have solved similar problems. Engineers often perform experiments related to the product they want to design.

For your model car, you could look at cars that are similar to the one you want to design. You might do research on the Internet. You could also test some materials to see whether they will work well in a model car.

Design a Solution

Brainstorm Ideas When engineers design new products, they usually work in teams. Design teams often hold brainstorming meetings in which any team member can contribute ideas. Brainstorming is a creative process in which one team member's suggestions often spark ideas in other group members. Brainstorming can lead to new approaches to solving a design problem.

Document the Process As the design team works, its members document, or keep a record of, the process. Having access to documentation enables others to repeat, or replicate, the process in the future. Design teams document their research sources, ideas, lists of materials, and so on because any part of the process may be a helpful resource later.

Identify Constraints During brainstorming, a design team may come up with several possible designs. To better focus their ideas, team members consider constraints. A constraint is a factor that limits a product design. Physical characteristics, such as the properties of materials used to make your model car, are constraints. Money and time are also constraints. If the materials in a product cost a lot or if the product takes a long time to make, the design may be impractical.

Make Trade-offs Design teams usually need to make trade-offs. In a trade-off, engineers give up one benefit of a proposed design in order to obtain another. In designing your model car, you might have to make trade-offs. For example, you might decide to give up the benefit of sturdiness in order to obtain the benefit of lower cost.

Select a Solution After considering the constraints and trade-offs of the possible designs, engineers then select one idea to develop further. That idea represents the solution that the team thinks best meets the need or solves the problem that was identified at the beginning of the process. The decision includes selecting the materials that will be used in the first attempt to build a product.

Build, Test, and Evaluate a Prototype

Once the team has chosen a design plan, the engineers build a prototype. A prototype is a working model used to test a design. Engineers evaluate the prototype to see whether it meets the goal. They must determine whether it works well, is easy to operate, is safe to use, and holds up to repeated use.

Part of the evaluation includes collecting data in the form of measurements. For example, think of your model car. Once you decide how to build your prototype, what would you want to know about it? You might want to measure how much baggage it could carry or how its shape affects its speed.

Communicate the Solution

A team needs to communicate the final design to the people who will manufacture and use the product. To do this, teams may use sketches, detailed drawings, computer simulations, and written descriptions. The team may also present the evidence that was collected when the prototype was tested. This evidence may include mathematical representations, such as graphs and data tables, that support the choice for the final design.

Troubleshoot and Redesign

Few prototypes work perfectly, which is why they need to be tested. Once a design team has tested a prototype, the members analyze the results and identify any problems. The team then tries to troubleshoot, or fix, the design problems. Troubleshooting allows the team to redesign the prototype to improve on how well the solution meets the need.

Science, Technology, Engineering, and Math

In your school, you probably have separate math, science, social studies, and English classes. Does that mean that you'll never use English in your math class or knowledge of geography in your science class? No! It turns out that the knowledge and skills you learn in one class or subject area will help you in other areas as well. This is especially true in the areas of STEM: Science, Technology, Engineering, and Math.

Science tries to understand the natural world and discover new knowledge. Engineers then use that knowledge to create solutions to problems through the development or use of technologies. Technology, engineering, and even math all work with science to expand our knowledge of the world around us.

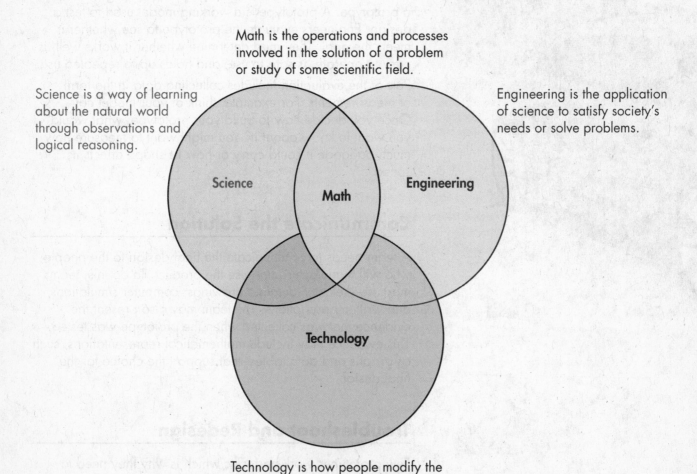

Math is the operations and processes involved in the solution of a problem or study of some scientific field.

Science is a way of learning about the natural world through observations and logical reasoning.

Engineering is the application of science to satisfy society's needs or solve problems.

Science

Math

Engineering

Technology

Technology is how people modify the world around them to meet their needs or to solve practical problems.

Scientific Inquiry Process and Engineering Design Process

Scientists and engineers use similar structured processes to do their work. These processes allow the scientists and engineers to work through questions or problems. Even if you're not a scientist or an engineer, these processes might help you answer a question or solve a problem!

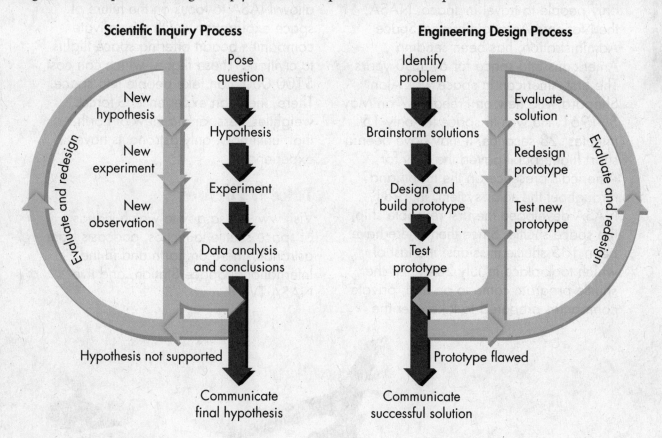

Scientific Inquiry Process

Pose question

New hypothesis

New experiment

New observation

Evaluate and redesign

Hypothesis

Experiment

Data analysis and conclusions

Hypothesis not supported

Communicate final hypothesis

Engineering Design Process

Identify problem

Evaluate solution

Redesign prototype

Test new prototype

Evaluate and redesign

Brainstorm solutions

Design and build prototype

Test prototype

Prototype flawed

Communicate successful solution

Space Exploration

Once upon a time, astronauts were the only people to travel in space. NASA, the National Aeronautics and Space Administration, has been sending Americans into space for over 50 years. The first American in space was Alan Shepard who flew on Freedom 7 on May 5, 1961. He was in space for only 15 minutes, 28 seconds. It may have been a short flight, but it paved the way for America's presence on the moon and throughout the solar system. In 1981, NASA developed the first reusable ship, the space shuttle. Since then, there have been 135 shuttle missions, the last of which took place in July 2011. As the shuttle program came to an end, private companies prepared to take over the development of space vehicles and allow NASA to focus on the future of space exploration. With this, private companies began offering space flights to civilians. These flights, which can cost $100,000, can take people into space. There, they can experience G-forces, weightlessness, and a view of Earth that, until now, only astronauts have experienced.

Take it Further

Visit www.nasa.gov to watch videos of space shuttle launches, podcasts from astronauts here on Earth and in the International Space Station, and live NASA TV.

SpaceShipTwo, the world's first commercial spaceship got a new look in May 2011. On its seventh flight since it was first launched in 2009, SpaceShipTwo released from its carrier at 51,500 feet. The entire trip, from the time SpaceShipTwo released from its carrier to the time it stopped on the runway lasted 11 minutes, 5 seconds!

Tourists in Space?

With new technology come new careers. What kinds of people will be needed to work in the space tourism industry? Obviously, with space tourism will come the need to build space vehicles. This will call for engineers, mechanics, and technicians who can ensure a safe, enjoyable ride to space. There will also be a need for pilots and astronauts, and trainers to prepare tourists for the demands of space travel. Aside from education and job-specific skills, companies such as the Spaceship Company, are looking for more. This company is looking for people who are self-motivated and able to work independently. They are looking for team players who can communicate well. To work in the space tourism industry, you will have to be able to work well under pressure, and accept challenges and responsibility. Is this you? Perhaps you have a future in the space tourism industry!

Take It Further

Use the Internet to research pioneers in the space tourism industry, such as Sir Richard Branson. Create a video or slideshow presentation that shows why you are qualified to work in the space tourism industry.

NASA's space shuttle program has delivered humans and supplies to space for over 50 years. In July 2011, four astronauts were sent on a 12-day mission to deliver supplies and spare parts to the International Space Station.

Space Travel for Everyone

Many adults can tell you where they were when the first Americans landed on the moon. Space travel has affected the lives of Americans. Because of NASA's work, we now know more about the universe than anyone before us even dreamed of knowing. The work of astronauts has increased our understanding of Earth and caused a technological explosion. The advent of satellites has allowed us to develop and use cell phones, satellite television, GPS, and other modern technologies. While NASA continues to study our universe, private companies are beginning to offer space travel to civilians. How will this affect society? The first space flights cost about $95,000, which makes them available to only the very wealthy. Does this mean that the average person will never experience the thrill of viewing Earth from space? Not necessarily. In the late 1930s, when airlines began carrying people across the country, most Americans couldn't afford to fly. It wasn't until the 1980s that air travel became affordable to the average American. Perhaps in 40 or 50 years, space flight will become as common as air travel.

Take It Further

The U.S. space program is over 50 years old. Much research has been done to understand how traveling in space affects the human body. Use the Internet to research the health effects of space travel on humans. Create a paper or digital brochure highlighting the effect of space travel on the human body.

The Douglas DC-3 helped to introduce air travel to the American people in 1935. Today, the XCOR Lynx suborbital vehicle is one of the first commercial space vehicles. Perhaps the Lynx will help make space travel a normal part of American life in the future.

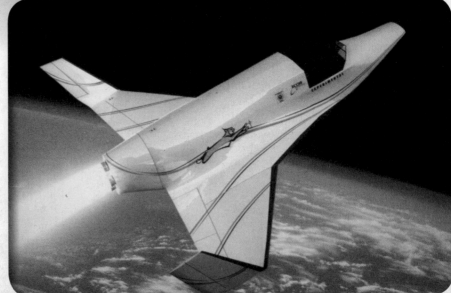

Name _____ Date _____ Class _____

Quick Lab History of Rockets

The science behind rockets and how they work hasn't changed much since the 1100s, but the designs and uses of rockets have. In this activity, you will build a simple rocket.

Inquiry Focus Build a Prototype

Materials tap water, empty 2-L soda bottle, poster board, scissors, tape or hot glue gun, rocket launcher and tire pump, stopwatch

Procedure

1. You and your partner will design and build a water rocket using the materials provided by your teacher. Your rocket must:
   - be made from an empty 2-L soda bottle.
   - have fins and a nose cone.
   - use air or a mixture of water and air as a propulsion system.
   - be launched on the class rocket launcher.
   - remain in the air for at least 5 seconds.

2. ✂ Consider the best shape for fins, and decide how many fins your rocket needs. Use poster board to make your fins.

3. Decide how much, if any, water to put in your rocket.

4. 🔥 After your teacher approves your design, build your rocket.

5. Test your rocket by launching it on the rocket launcher provided by your teacher. Use a stopwatch to time how long your rocket remains in the air. **CAUTION:** *Make sure that the rocket is launched vertically in a safe, open area that is at least 30 m across. All observers should wear safety goggles and stay at least 8–10 m away from the rocket launcher. The rocket should be pumped to a pressure of no more than 50 pounds per square inch.*

Think It Over

1. Look at all the different rockets designed by the class. How are the rocket designs similar? How are they different?

   _____

   _____

2. Was your rocket able to stay in the air for at least 5 seconds? What changes might you make in the rocket's design to improve its performance?

   _____

   _____

Building Space Vehicles

Copyright © Pearson Education, Inc., or its affiliates. All rights reserved.

Vocabulary Practice

Use your textbook or a dictionary to define the science, technology, engineering, and math terms in the chart below. Complete the chart by writing a strategy to help you remember the meaning of each term. One has been done for you.

Term	Definition	How I'm going to remember the meaning
rocket		
thrust		
velocity		
space probe	a spacecraft that has various scientific instruments that can collect data, including visual images, but has no human crew	*Probe* means to "check out." So, a space probe is a machine that checks out space.
space spinoff		
solar system		
terrestrial planet		
gas giant		
optical engineer		
rate		

Building Space Vehicles

Converting Measures

To convert units of measure and rates, multiply by ratios that are equal to 1. The ratios relate different units of measure. Unit analysis is used to check that the unit conversion is correct.

Example 1   Convert 1,900,000 kHz to megahertz.

Step 1 Use the conversion equation to write a ratio equivalent to 1. Write the unit you want to find as the first term.

$$\frac{1 \text{ MHz}}{1,000 \text{ kHz}} = 1$$

Step 2 Multiply.

$$1,900,000 \text{ kHz} \times \frac{1 \text{ MHz}}{1,000 \text{ kHz}} = \frac{1,900,000 \text{ MHz}}{1,000} = 1,900 \text{ MHz}$$

So, 1,900,000 kHz = 1,900 MHz.

Conversion Equations

100 cm = 1 m	1,000 kHz = 1 MHz
1,000 m = 1 km	1,000 mg = 1 g
1.61 km = 1 mi	0.26 gal = 1 L

Example 2   Convert 10 m/s to kilometers per hour.

Step 1 Write ratios equal to 1 that relate seconds to minutes, minutes to hours, and kilometers to meters.

$$\frac{60 \text{ s}}{1 \text{ min}} = 1 \qquad \frac{60 \text{ min}}{1 \text{ h}} = 1 \qquad \frac{1 \text{ km}}{1,000 \text{ m}} = 1$$

Step 2 Convert seconds to hours and meters to kilometers. Multiply using equivalent ratios. Cancel units.

$$\frac{10 \text{ m}}{\text{s}} \times \frac{60 \text{ s}}{1 \text{ min}} \times \frac{60 \text{ min}}{1 \text{ h}} \times \frac{1 \text{ km}}{1,000 \text{ m}} = \frac{36,000 \text{ km}}{1,000 \text{ h}} \text{ or } \frac{36 \text{ km}}{1 \text{ h}}$$

So, 10 m/s = 36 km/h.

TRY IT YOURSELF!

Convert. Use the table of conversion equations to help.

1. 5.5 mi = ☐ km

$$5.5 \text{ mi} \times \frac{1.61 \text{ km}}{1 \text{ mi}} = \boxed{} \text{ km}$$

2. 40 L = ☐ gal

$$40 \text{ L} \times \frac{\boxed{} \text{ gal}}{\boxed{} \text{ L}} = \boxed{} \text{ L}$$

3. 25 mg = ☐ g

4. 52 mi/gal = ☐ km/L

5. 280 mi/h = ☐ km/h

6. 12 cm/s = ☐ m/min

Converting Measures Calculating Distances in Space

Distances in space are so large that meters and kilometers are not very practical units. Scientists often use astronomical units (AU) to measure distances within the solar system. They use light-years to measure distances to stars. The following equations show the relationships between these units of measurement.

1 AU = 150,000,000 km (approximately)   1 light-year = 63,241 AU

Sample Problem: When Earth is closest to Mars, the distance is around 0.374 AU. What is the distance in kilometers?

1. Read and Understand

What information is given? (the distance between Earth and Mars, 0.374 AU, and the relationship between AU and kilometers)
What are you asked to find? (the distance in kilometers)

2. Plan and Solve

Use unit analysis. 0.374 AU = ☐ km

Write a ratio equivalent to 1 to relate astronomical units to kilometers.
Use kilometers as the first term. $\dfrac{150,000,000 \text{ km}}{1 \text{ AU}}$

Multiply the ratio by the distance, 0.374 AU, and cancel units.

$0.374 \text{ A̶U̶} \times \dfrac{150,000,000 \text{ km}}{1 \text{ A̶U̶}} = 0.374 \times 150,000,000 \text{ km}$

Simplify.   0.374 AU = 56,100,000 km

3. Look Back and Check

Is the answer reasonable? (Yes; $0.4 \times 150,000,000$ is 60,000,000, which is close to the answer, and the unit analysis is correct.)

TRY IT YOURSELF! ●

1. The mean distance between Jupiter and the sun is 5.203 AU. What is this distance in kilometers?

2. The distance from Mercury to the sun varies between 0.307 AU and 0.467 AU. What is the difference between these distances expressed in kilometers?

3. The distance from the sun to Alpha Centauri, the closest star system, is 4.3 light-years. What is the distance in astronomical units?

4. The star Arcturus is about 37 light-years from Earth. What is the distance in kilometers?

Building Space Vehicles

Career Spotlight Optical Engineer

Did you realize that one of the most important pieces of scientific and engineering equipment on the Mars Rover are its cameras? In fact, there are four types of camera: the PanCam, which is for remote sensing; the NavCam, which helps direct the rover as it drives across Mars; the HazCam, which contains fish-eye lenses; and the Microscopic Imager for close-ups. Each camera contains lenses that are small, simple, and that survived getting to Mars and driving on Mars. Refer to the Technology Zone on page 11S to see one type of space probe.

An optical engineer designed each of the lenses. Optical engineers are experts in the science of optics. They use their knowledge of optics to solve problems such as designing and building cameras that transmit images and are able to survive harsh conditions on distant planets.

This requires them to understand and apply the science of optics in order to know what is physically possible for a camera lens to do as well as what is practical in terms of available technology, materials, and design methods.

The "six-wheeled robotic geologists" are still transmitting information to scientists on Earth because the cameras and lenses are still healthy and active.

Design It

Work with a partner. Use the Internet to research space probes and their cameras. Think about a rover that you'd like to send to a distant planet. In the space below, draw the rover, and include at least four cameras. Label each camera and write the objective for each camera.

STEM Project Space Exploration Vehicle

How can you design a vehicle that will be used on the surface of a moon or planet that you have never visited? You already know the requirements of a vehicle that is used on Earth's surface. If you know about the landscape of the planet or moon and the purpose of the vehicle, you can design, build, and test a vehicle for the exploration of the planet or moon.

For this project, you will use the information you have learned about the different types of landscapes found on the planets and moons in our solar system. You will then use that knowledge to design and build a vehicle that can navigate the varied terrains. Refer to the Engineering Design Process flowchart in the middle of the book if you need help.

Project Rules

- Identify the landscapes and geological features that are found on the planets and moons of the solar system.
- Brainstorm ways to build a vehicle that can overcome these terrains while carrying equipment.
- Design and sketch a model of the vehicle.
- Build a model vehicle.
- Present the vehicle to the class, and test it.

Suggested Materials

You will need design tools such as rulers, scissors, glue, and so on. Prototypes can be built from simple materials such as cardboard, foam board, and craft sticks. Wooden dowels may be helpful for wheel axles.

Attach a long string to each vehicle so that it can be pulled across the test course. If you are testing the vehicles in the classroom, a test course can be made by placing obstacles such as books, boxes, and rugs on the floor.

Name _____ Date _____ Class _____

Project Hints

You will work on the project in small groups. First, focus on a small number of planets or moons to identify landscapes. After each group makes a list of potential landscapes, get together as a class to make a combined list. Then, with the class, eliminate those planets and moons with landscapes that cannot be navigated by a vehicle, such as the gas giants. Then, because it will be difficult to design for all possible landscape features, you may either choose a few of the identified landscape features as a design goal or choose a particular planet or moon on which to focus. As an alternative, if your teacher has designated a "test site" (for example, a playground), you can design for this site. Work with your group to brainstorm, design, and build a vehicle that will work well in your chosen landscape.

Project Timeline

Task	Due Date
1. Research planets and satellites.	_____
2. List possible landscapes to explore.	_____
3. Identify design requirements for the exploration vehicle.	_____
4. Sketch the design on paper.	_____
5. Make a prototype vehicle.	_____
6. Test and present the vehicle.	_____

Building Space Vehicles

Project Worksheet 1

Solar System Landscapes

Planets and Major Moons	Description of Planet or Moon	Landscapes—Check all that exist on the planet or moon.							
		Dirt or Gravel	Rocks	Ice	Craters	Volcanoes/Geysers	Cliffs/Cracks	Bodies of Water or Other Liquid	Other (Please explain.)
Mercury									
Venus									
Earth									
Moon									
Mars									
Phobos									
Deimos									
Jupiter									
Io									
Europa									
Ganymede									
Callisto									
Saturn									
Titan									
Uranus									
Miranda									
Neptune									
Triton									
Pluto									
Charon									

Building Space Vehicles

Name _____   Date _____   Class _____

Project Worksheet 2
Vehicle Design

1. List the types of landscapes that your vehicle may encounter on your chosen planet or moon.

_____

_____

_____

_____

_____

2. List your design requirements. Be as specific as you can, and explain how the requirements relate to the landscapes that you may encounter.

_____

_____

_____

_____

_____

3. Make a sketch of your vehicle. Be sure to include enough details and explanations of special features to allow others to understand your drawing.

Name _____ Date _____ Class _____

Space Exploration Vehicle

In evaluating how well you complete the STEM Project, your teacher will judge your work in four categories. In each, a score of 4 is the best rating.

	4	3	2	1
Developing List of Design Requirements	List specifically describes the landscape that the vehicle will need to travel over and thoroughly explains how the requirements for the vehicle design relate to the landscape.	List includes a fairly detailed description of the landscape that the vehicle will need to travel over and provides a good explanation of how the requirements for the vehicle design relate to the landscape.	List includes a general description of the landscape that the vehicle will need to travel over and provides an explanation that shows some understanding of how the requirements for the vehicle design relate to the landscape.	List includes a limited description of the landscape that the vehicle will need to travel over and provides an explanation that shows a limited understanding of how the requirements for the vehicle design relate to the landscape.
Creating Sketches of Vehicle	Sketches show originality of design and a thorough understanding of the requirements of the terrain.	Sketches show some originality of design and a good understanding of the requirements of the terrain.	Sketches show an adequate design and some understanding of the requirements of the terrain.	Sketches show an incomplete or inappropriate design and little or no understanding of the requirements of the terrain.
Constructing Model of Vehicle	Model is well constructed and includes all design requirements.	Model is adequately constructed and includes all design requirements.	Model is adequately constructed and includes some but not all design requirements.	Model is inadequately constructed or does not include all design requirements.
Presenting the Model to the Class	Presentation is thorough and interesting and includes a clear, accurate explanation of how the vehicle meets its design requirements.	Presentation is fairly thorough and includes a satisfactory explanation of how the vehicle meets its design requirements.	Presentation is not thorough. Includes a partial explanation of how the vehicle meets its design requirements.	Presentation includes an incomplete or inaccurate explanation of how the vehicle meets its design requirements.
Participating in the Group	Takes a lead in planning, constructing, and presenting the vehicle.	Participates in all aspects of planning, constructing, and presenting the vehicle.	Participates in most aspects of planning, constructing, and presenting the vehicle.	Plays a minor role in planning, constructing, and presenting the vehicle.

Technology Zone What Are Space Probes?

Since space exploration began in the 1950s, only 24 people have traveled as far as the moon. No one has traveled farther. Yet, during this period, space scientists have gathered a great deal of information about other parts of the solar system. This information was collected by space probes. A space probe is a spacecraft that carries scientific instruments that can collect data but has no human crew.

Each space probe is designed for a specific mission. Some probes are designed to land on a certain planet. Others are designed to fly by and collect data about more than one planet.

Each space probe has a power system to produce electricity and a communication system to send and receive signals. Probes also carry scientific instruments to collect data and perform experiments. Some probes, called **orbiters,** are equipped to photograph and analyze the atmosphere of a planet. Other probes, called **landers,** are equipped to land on a planet and analyze the materials on its surface. Some have small robots called **rovers** that move around on the surface. A rover typically has instruments that collect and analyze soil and rock samples.

In 2005, NASA's *Cassini* orbiter sent back evidence that one of Saturn's moons, *Enceladus,* might have liquid water and the right amount of heat to support life.

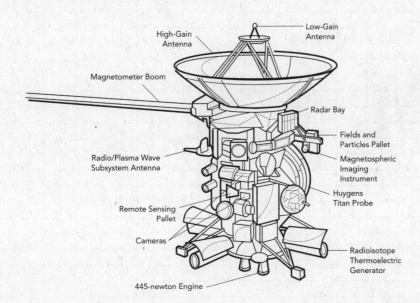

Design It

Working with a partner, you will design a space probe. Using the following questions as a guide, brainstorm and discuss your ideas with your partner before you begin your design.

1. Which planet or moon do you want to send a probe to and why?

2. What is the objective of the probe?

3. Which instruments does your probe need to accomplish the objective?

4. What kind of radiation protection and temperature control does your probe need?

5. Now draw your probe on the next page. Be sure to label your power devices and scientific instruments.

Building Space Vehicles

Ideas, Drawings, and Answers

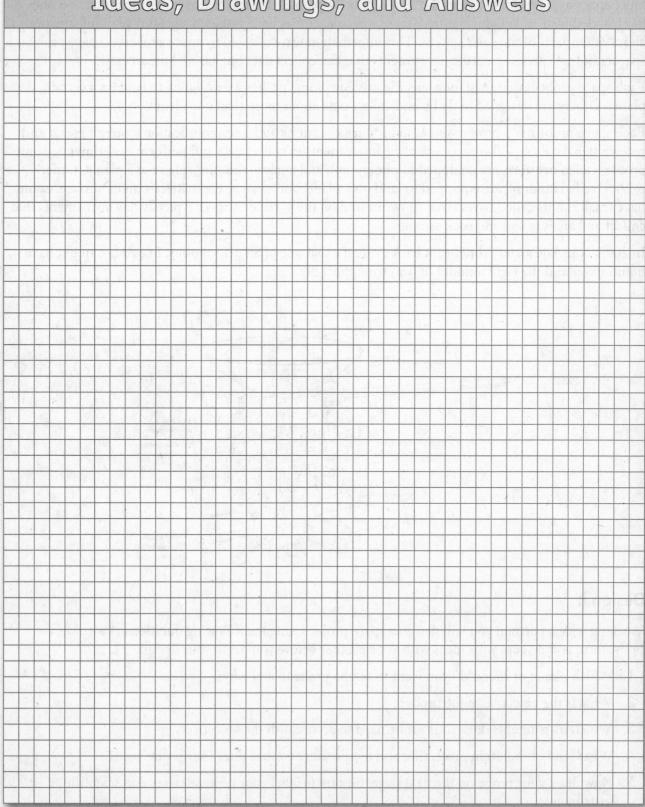

☐ = 1 cm

Building Space Vehicles

PRE LAB

Space Spinoffs

Reviewing Content

A space spinoff is an item or a material that was originally developed for the space program and is now used on Earth. To date, thousands of spinoffs exist. Many of these spinoffs are in products you use every day. One spinoff is a thin aluminum coating developed by NASA. This coating is now used to make special blankets. Campers, hikers, and hunters use these blankets to keep themselves dry and warm when outdoors. Such blankets are also used in the medical field to prevent shock that can occur from an accident or exposure to cold weather conditions. The spinoff blankets are paper-thin and weigh only about 300 grams. They can even be folded up to fit into the pocket of a pair of pants!

Many of these blankets, called thermal survival blankets, look like ponchos with hoods, as shown above. The innermost layer of the blanket has an extremely reflective coating, which reflects and holds as much as 80 percent of the body heat given off by the wearer. Thus, the blankets are thermal insulators. A thermal insulator is a material that does not allow heat to pass through easily.

Reviewing Inquiry Focus

In order to develop effective thermal survival blankets, scientists tested different materials to see how well each acted as a thermal insulator. In this Lab Investigation, you will test the insulating capacity of aluminum foil to simulate how it works in thermal survival blankets. You will graph your results and draw various conclusions from your data.

1. Read the procedure for this Lab Investigation. How will you determine if the foil is a good thermal insulator?

   _____

   _____

2. What type of graph will you be making from your data?

   _____

   _____

Hands-on Inquiry Space Spinoffs

Problem How does a blanket protect against heat loss?

Inquiry Focus Design an Experiment, Draw Conclusions

Materials foil blanket piece, cloth blanket piece, 3 thermometers, 600-mL beaker, ice cubes, 3 identical small test tubes, 3 identical large test tubes, cotton balls, transparent adhesive tape or rubber bands, stopwatch or watch with second hand

Design an Experiment

1. Imagine that you are a scientist working for a camping equipment company. You have been asked to conduct a study on the effectiveness of different materials for emergency blankets. You have been asked to test which blanket holds heat better over time.

2. Start by making observations about the two different types of blankets. Make a data table on the next page, and record observations about the thickness, texture, water resistance, and other properties of the two blankets.

3. Make a prediction about which blanket will hold heat better. Write your prediction and reasoning below.

_____

_____

4. Using the materials provided, design an experiment to test your prediction. You will need to not only compare the two blankets, but also compare them with an experimental setup that has no blanket. You will need to:

   • wrap two of the small test tubes in the two different types of blankets, leaving another small test tube without a covering.

   • half-fill the small test tubes with hot water and insert a thermometer into each.

   • use ice water in the beaker to compare the effectiveness of the blankets.

   In your groups, discuss how you will use materials to:

   • attach the blankets to the small test tubes.

   • keep both blankets dry.

   • seal off the tops of the small test tubes with the thermometers inside.

   • compare the changes in temperature in your different experimental setups.

5. In the space provided, write a detailed procedure for your investigation and create a data table for your observations and results. If you need additional space, use the next page.

Procedure

_____

_____

_____

_____

_____

_____

_____

_____

_____

Data Table

6. 🗒️ 🔥 📋 Have your teacher approve your procedure and data table. Then carry out your experiment.

Ideas, Drawings, and Answers

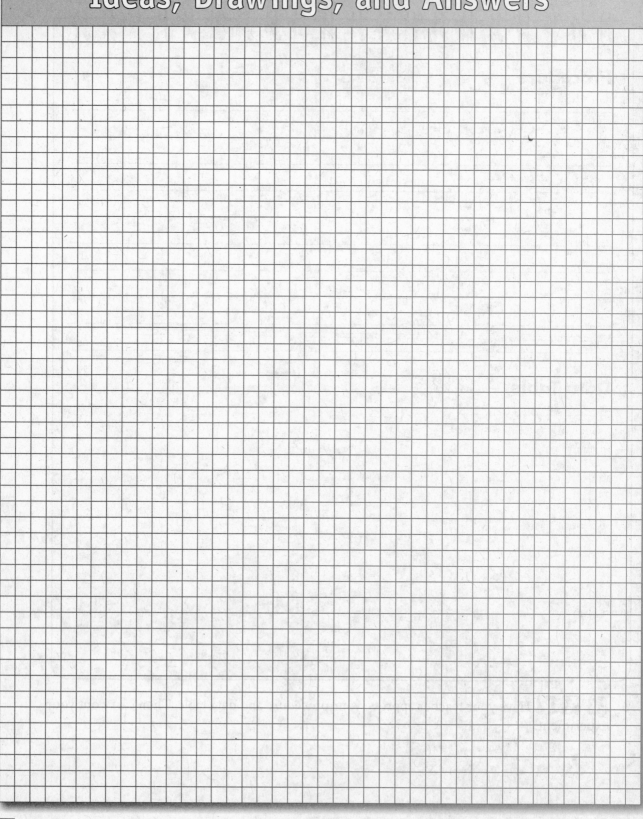

$\square$ = 1 cm

Building Space Vehicles

Analyze and Conclude

1. **Design an Experiment** What was the purpose of the third, unwrapped test tube setup?

   _____

   _____

   _____

   _____

2. **Draw Conclusions** If the small test tube had more contact with the large test tube, so that the heat being lost was through conduction, which material do you think would perform better? Explain.

   _____

   _____

   _____

   _____

3. **Observe** Calculate the differences between the initial and final temperatures in all three test tubes. Which thermometer registered the greatest temperature change? Which registered the least?

   _____

   _____

   _____

4. **Interpret Data** Which type of blanket prevented heat loss more effectively? Explain.

   _____

   _____

   _____

   _____

5. **Identify a Need** Suppose you are a scientist for a national camping equipment company. What factors do you need to consider when designing a blanket other than preventing heat loss?

   _____

   _____

   _____

Building Space Vehicles

POST LAB

Space Spinoffs

1. **Analyze Sources of Error** What sources of error might have affected your results? How?

_____

_____

_____

2. **Evaluate Scientific Claims** As an employee of a camping equipment company, can you truthfully claim that the foil blanket will help keep someone warm? Explain why or why not.

_____

_____

_____

3. **Infer** Regardless of which blanket traps heat better, what might be an advantage of the foil blanket?

_____

_____

_____

4. **Summarize** Describe what you learned in this lab about how the space spinoffs known as thermal survival blankets work and what questions you still have.

What I learned _____

_____

What I still want to know _____

_____

Communicate

Demonstrate Consumer Literacy Write an advertisement on the next page for the blanket that proved to be the better insulator. In the ad, describe the test procedures that you used to justify your claim. Also explain why this particular blanket would benefit consumers. Be prepared to share your advertisement with the class.

Name _____ Date _____ Class _____

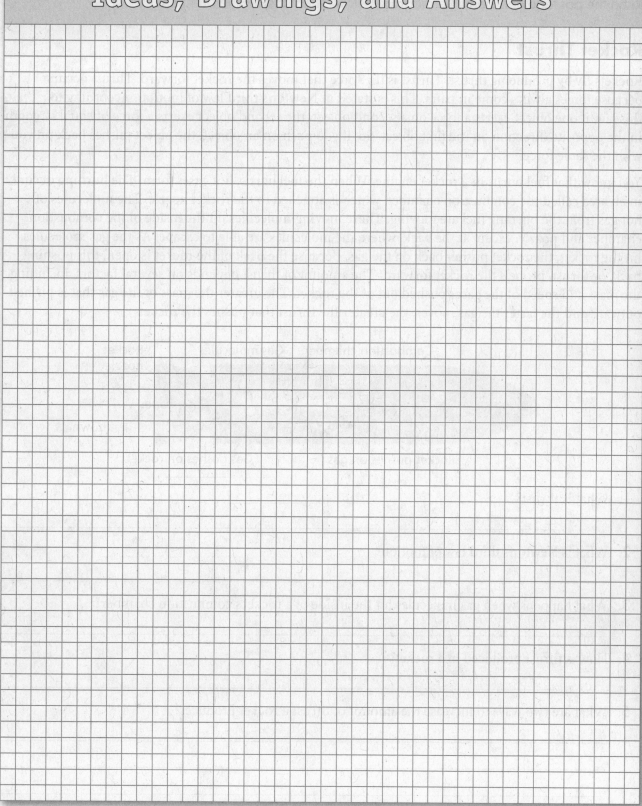

Ideas, Drawings, and Answers

☐ = 1 cm

Building Space Vehicles

Enrichment The Science of Rockets

Read the passage and study the diagram below. Then answer the questions.

Rocket Thrust

Rockets fly by producing thrust. Thrust is the force that moves the rocket forward. Thrust occurs because forces always come in pairs. This is stated in Newton's third law of motion. According to this law, if one object exerts a force on a second object, the second object exerts a force of equal strength in the opposite direction on the first object. So, if you push on an object, the object pushes back on you with the same force.

You know that fuel burns in a rocket engine. When the fuel burns, hot gases form. The burning occurs in an area called the combustion chamber, which is attached to the rocket nozzle. The molecules of hot gas from the burning fuel are moving. These moving molecules hit the inside of the combustion chamber and nozzle, except at the back, where the molecules are able to escape. As the gas molecules hit the rocket, the rocket pushes back on the gas. Because the back of the rocket is open, this pushing back, or thrust, propels the rocket forward. The amount of thrust depends on several factors, including the mass and speed of the gases pushed out of the rocket. The greater the mass of the gas that is pushed outward and the faster the gas moves, the greater the thrust that pushes the rocket.

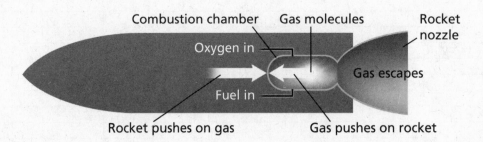

1. What is thrust?

_____

2. What is Newton's third law of motion?

_____

3. What happens when gas molecules hit the inside of a rocket's combustion chamber?

_____

4. How is thrust produced in a rocket?

_____

5. What are two ways to increase the amount of thrust a rocket produces?

_____

_____

Building Space Vehicles

Assessment Building Space Vehicles

Fill in the blank to complete each statement.

1. A spacecraft that has various scientific instruments that can collect data but does not have a human crew is called a(n) _____.

2. Some probes have small robots called _____ that can move about on the surface of another planet or moon.

3. A _____ is a group of parts that work together as a whole.

4. _____ is the name often given to the four inner planets: Mercury, Venus, Earth, and Mars.

5. A _____ is a ratio that compares two quantities measured in different units.

If the statement is true, write *true*. If the statement is false, change the underlined word or words to make the statement true.

6. _____ Probes called <u>rovers</u> are equipped to photograph and analyze the atmosphere of a planet.

7. _____ A <u>structural</u> engineer designs and builds cameras that transmit images.

8. _____ <u>Gas giant</u> is the name often given to the outer planets: Jupiter, Saturn, Uranus, and Neptune.

? What technologies are needed to explore terrains on other planets?

9. Suppose you are planning a Mars mission. What types of technology would be beneficial to gather information on your mission?

_____

_____

_____

_____

_____

_____

Name _____ Date _____ Class _____

Performance Assessment Asteroid Smasher

Purpose To examine how thrust and launch angle affect a rocket's course

Materials
- wooden pencil (unsharpened)
- pencil-cap eraser
- piece of wire or paper clip
- tape (adhesive or masking)
- small pieces of poster board for fins
- coping saw or mat knife
- flat file
- pliers
- rubber bands
- target, 1 foot in diameter

Scenario

Suppose you woke up tomorrow to find this article on the front page of your newspaper:

GIANT ASTEROID HEADED STRAIGHT FOR EARTH!

White House to Build Rocket

WASHINGTON, D.C.—In an early-morning press conference, the President confirmed reports that NASA scientists have discovered a large asteroid headed for Earth. Experts believe that the asteroid, called 2045DD, will collide with our planet in about six months.

The President reassured the panicked nation that plans are underway to build a rocket that will deliver a bomb to the asteroid. The explosion should break the asteroid apart, or at least change its course so that it misses Earth.

A team of engineers was seen entering the Oval Office shortly after the President's announcement. A source close to the President was overheard saying that the Commander in Chief isn't sure that the plan will work, but others speculate that, if designed correctly,

(story continued on page A2)

As aerospace engineers (rocket scientists), you and your partners know that a rocket carrying a bomb could destroy or change the direction of the asteroid. The President of the United States is skeptical. Therefore, the White House has asked your team to build an inexpensive model of the rocket to demonstrate its accuracy and reliability. Your final objective is to stop the asteroid before it strikes Earth, but first you must convince the President and Congress to fund the project.

You and your partners will work together to build and test a model rocket. You may find building the model easy, but the hard part is making sure your rocket can hit its target every time. You must test several variables, including the speed of the rocket, angle of launch, and distance to the target. You know that you should only test one variable at a time and keep all other variables constant. Your rocket would only get one chance to destroy an approaching asteroid, so the President is only going to watch one demonstration. You have to hit your target! If you fail, Earth may be doomed!

Procedure

1. **Building a Rocket** Follow the directions from NASA to build a pencil rocket.

2. **The Best Combination** A rocket's course is influenced by the angle of launch, the amount of thrust (number of rubber bands), and the distance to the target. The distance to the target is set. The other variables are not. Use the launch pad provided by your teacher to test one variable at a time, and record all trials in a data table. Your goal is to find the best combination of launch angle and thrust so that your rocket hits a one-foot-diameter target at a distance of 30 feet every time it's launched.

3. **Plan Well** Because you are sharing the launch pad with other companies, you will only be allowed ten launches to test the variables.

4. **The Big Day** You will only get one chance to impress the President of the United States. Use the best combination of angle and thrust you found during your tests. Give it your best shot!

Conclusion

Let's see what you have learned about rockets.

1. Rubber bands provided the thrust to get your rocket going. Why did the rocket keep moving after it left the launch pad and the rubber bands were no longer pushing it?

   _____
   _____

2. How did the launch angle affect the distance the rocket traveled?

   _____
   _____

3. What happens when a rocket reaches escape velocity?

   _____
   _____

4. Is the pencil rocket really a rocket? Explain.

   _____
   _____

Whether or not you hit the target on the final test day, the White House officials want your written report. In it, they want the results of your tests. You should address the following questions in your report on the next page:

- What different thrust forces (number of rubber bands) did you test?
- What different launch angles did you test?
- What combination worked best, and did it work every time?
- What type of design do you suggest engineers use when they build the rocket?

23S
Building Space Vehicles

Name _____ Date _____ Class _____

Ideas, Drawings, and Answers

☐ = 1 cm

Building Space Vehicles

Standardized Test Prep

Multiple Choice

Circle the letter of the best answer.

1. The table below shows data for five planets.

Planet	Period of Rotation (Earth days)	Period of Revolution (Earth years)	Average Distance from the Sun (million km)
Mars	1.03	1.9	228
Jupiter	0.41	12	779
Saturn	0.45	29	1,434
Uranus	0.72	84	2,873
Neptune	0.67	164	4,495

According to the table, which planet has a "day" that is most similar in length to a day on Earth?

A   Mars   B   Jupiter

C   Neptune   D   Uranus

2. What characteristic do all of the outer planets share?

A   They have rocky surfaces.

B   They are larger than the sun.

C   They have many moons.

D   They have thin atmospheres.

3. Which type of numbers does scientific notation best describe?

A   very small or very large

B   very large only

C   very small only

D   large and small combined

4. When designing camera lenses for the Mars Rover, optical engineers need to consider which of the following factors?

A   cost

B   materials

C   environmental conditions

D   all of the above

Constructed Response

Use the tables to the right and your knowledge of science to help you answer Question 5.

5. Escape velocity is the velocity a rocket must reach to fly beyond a planet's gravitational pull. The table shows the escape velocity for a rocket leaving different objects in the solar system. Explain why it might be easier to launch a rocket to Mars from the moon rather than from Earth. What would be the problem with sending astronauts to explore Jupiter?

Object	Escape velocity (km/s)	Object	Escape velocity (km/s)
MERCURY	4.3	JUPITER	59.5
VENUS	10.3	SATURN	35.6
MOON	2.4	URANUS	21.2
MARS	5.0	NEPTUNE	23.6

_____

_____

_____

_____

_____

_____

_____

_____

25S

Building Space Vehicles

Collect and record your data.

Record observations and measurements you make during your experiment. Use a data table to organize and record your observations.

Interpret your data.

Organize your notes and records to make them clear. Make diagrams, charts, or graphs to help you analyze your data. Look for patterns or trends in your data.

State your conclusion.

Your conclusion is a statement that sums up what you have learned from your experiment. Communicate what you found out. Tell whether your data supported your hypothesis.

Try it again.

Repeat the experiment a few more times. The results of one experiment might not be correct. Be sure to repeat everything exactly the same each time.

Scientific Methods

In some ways, scientists are like detectives, piecing together clues to learn about a process or event. One way that scientists gather clues is by carrying out experiments. An experiment tests an idea in a careful, orderly manner.

Although experiments do not all follow the same steps in the same order, many follow a pattern similar to the one described here.

Pose a question.

Experiments begin by asking a question about an observation you make. A scientific question is one that can be answered by gathering evidence.

State your hypothesis.

A hypothesis is a possible answer to your question. It must be something that you can test with an experiment. Write it as an *If...then...because* statement.

Identify and Control Variables.

Variables are things that can change in your experiment. For a fair test, choose just one variable to change. Keep the other variables constant.

Test your hypothesis.

Make a plan to test your hypothesis. Write a step-by-step procedure. Collect materials and tools. Then follow your plan. Each time you test your hypothesis is called a trial. Repeat each trial multiple times.

Length

Length is measured in **meters (m)**. Length is the distance between two points. The distance from the floor to a doorknob is about one meter. Long distances are measured in kilometers (km). Short distances are measured in centimeters (cm) or millimeters (mm). Scientists use metric rulers and meter sticks to measure length.

Liquid Volume

Liquid volume is measured in **liters (L)**. Liquid volume is the amount of space a liquid takes up. One liter is about the volume of a medium-size milk container. Smaller volumes are measured in milliliters (mL). Scientists use graduated cylinders to measure liquid volume. The graduated cylinder to the right is marked with milliliter divisions. Notice that the water in the cylinder has a curved surface. This curved surface is called the meniscus. To measure the volume, you must read the level at the lowest point of the meniscus.

Time

Scientists measure time in **seconds (s)**.

Common Conversions		
1 km	=	1,000 m
1 m	=	100 cm
1 m	=	1,000 mm
1 cm	=	10 mm

This shell is 7.8 cm or 78 mm.

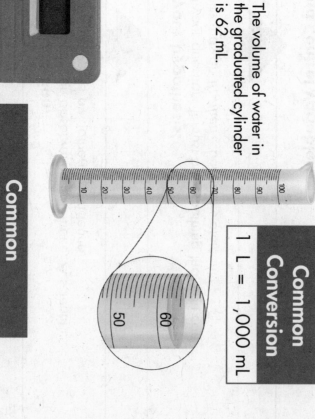

The volume of water in the graduated cylinder is 62 mL.

Common Conversion
1 L = 1,000 mL

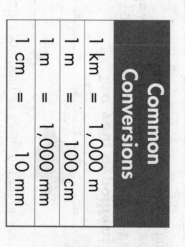

Common Conversions		
1 hour	=	60 minutes
1 minute	=	60 seconds

Making Measurements

Scientists use measurements to record precise observations. They also use measurements to communicate their findings.

Measuring in SI

Scientists use the **International System of Units (SI)** as their standard system of measurement. SI units are easy to use. Each unit is ten times greater than the next smallest unit. The table lists some SI prefixes. These prefixes name the most common SI units.

Mass

Mass is measured in **grams (g)**. Mass is the amount of matter in an object. One gram is about the mass of a paper clip. Larger masses are measured in kilograms (kg). Scientists use a balance to find the mass of an object.

Temperature

Scientists use the **Celsius scale** to measure temperature. Temperature is recorded in degrees Celsius (°C). Water freezes at 0°C and boils at 100°C. Scientists measure temperature using a thermometer.

The temperature of the water is 35°C.

Common SI Prefixes

Prefix	Symbol	Meaning
kilo-	k	1,000
hecto-	h	100
deca-	da	10
deci-	d	0.1 (one tenth)
centi-	c	0.01 (one hundredth)
milli-	m	0.001 (one thousandth)

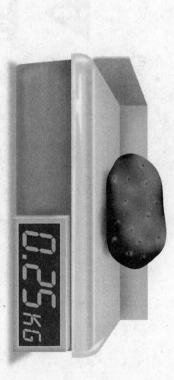

The mass of the potato is 0.25 kg or 250 g.

Common Conversion

1 kg = 1,000 g

Flames Before you work with flames, tie back loose hair and clothing. Follow instructions from your teacher about lighting and extinguishing flames.

 No Flames When using flammable materials, make sure there are no flames, sparks, or other exposed heat sources present.

 **Corrosive Chemical** Avoid getting acid or other corrosive chemicals on your skin or clothing or in your eyes. Do not inhale the vapors. Wash your hands after the activity.

 Poison Do not let any poisonous chemical come into contact with your skin, and do not inhale its vapors. Wash your hands when you are finished with the activity.

 Physical Safety When an experiment involves physical activity, avoid injuring yourself or others. Alert your teacher if there is any reason you should not participate.

 Disposal Dispose of chemicals and other laboratory materials safely. Follow the instructions from your teacher.

 Hand Washing Wash your hands thoroughly when finished with an activity. Use soap and warm water. Rinse well.

 General Safety Awareness When this symbol appears, follow the instructions provided. When you are asked to develop your own procedure in a lab, have your teacher approve your plan before you go further.

Safety Symbols

These symbols warn of possible dangers in the laboratory and remind you to work carefully.

 Safety Goggles Wear safety goggles to protect your eyes in any activity involving chemicals, flames or heating, or glassware.

 Lab Apron Wear a laboratory apron to protect your skin and clothing from damage.

 Breakage Handle breakable materials, such as glassware, with care. Do not touch broken glassware.

 Heat-Resistant Gloves Use an oven mitt or other hand protection when handling hot materials, such as hot plates or hot glassware.

 Plastic Gloves Wear disposable plastic gloves when working with harmful chemicals and organisms. Keep your hands away from your face, and dispose of the gloves according to your teacher's instructions.

 Heating Use a clamp or tongs to pick up hot glassware. Do not touch hot objects with your bare hands.

 Fumes Work in a well-ventilated area when harmful vapors may be involved. Avoid inhaling vapors directly. Only test an odor when directed to do so by your teacher, and use a wafting motion to direct the vapor toward your nose.

 Sharp Object Scissors, scalpels, knives, needles, pins, and tacks can cut your skin. Always direct a sharp edge or point away from yourself and others.

 Animal Safety Treat live or preserved animals or animal parts with care to avoid harming the animals or yourself. Wash your hands when you are finished with the activity.

 Plant Safety Handle plants only as directed by your teacher. If you are allergic to certain plants, tell your teacher; do not do an activity involving those plants. Avoid touching harmful plants, such as poison ivy. Wash your hands when you are finished with the activity.

 Electric Shock To avoid electric shock, never use electrical equipment around water, or when the equipment or your hands are wet. Be sure cords are untangled and cannot trip anyone. Unplug equipment not in use.

= 1 cm

STEM Glossary

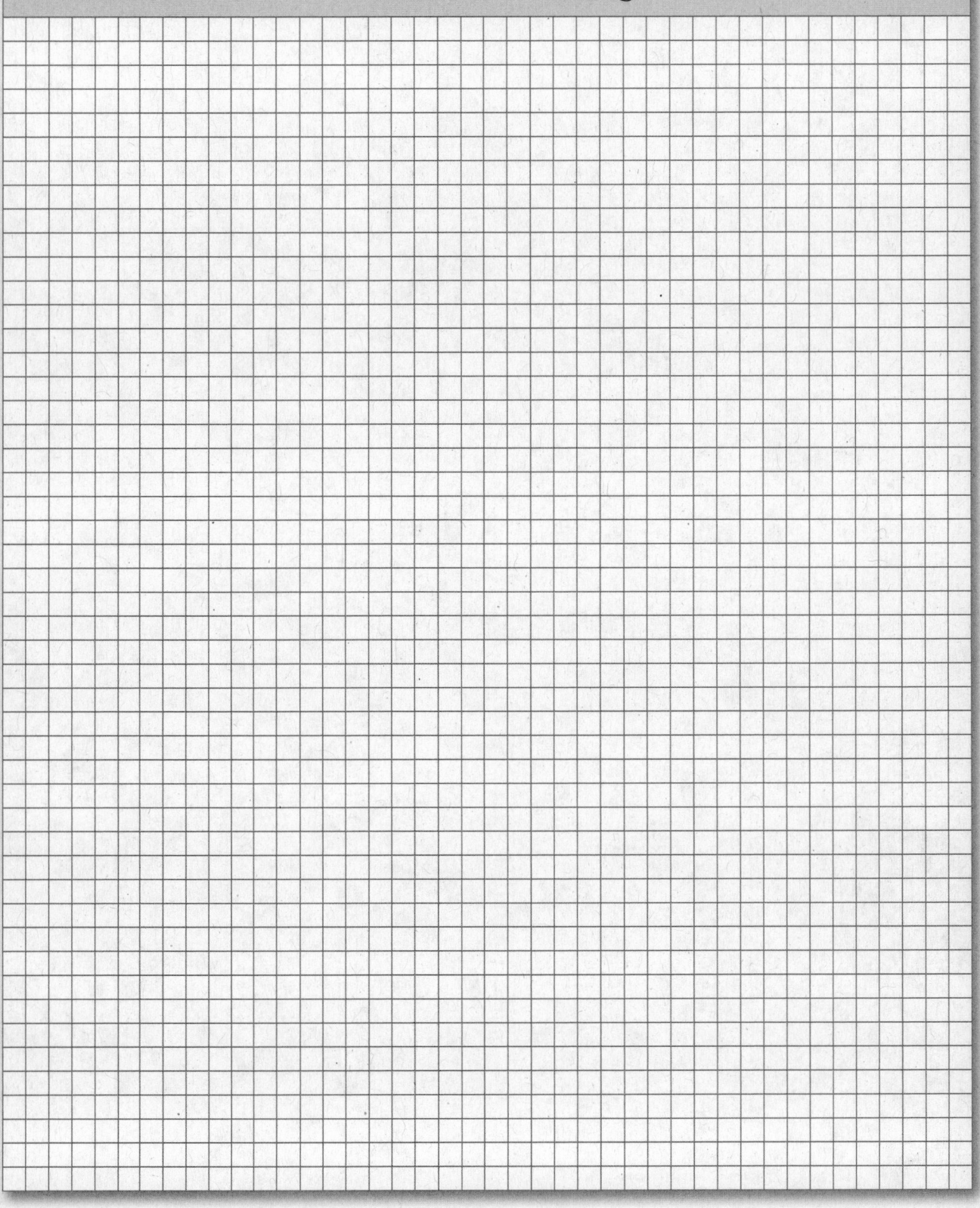

☐ = 1 cm

PROJECT
STEM

SCIENCE • TECHNOLOGY • ENGINEERING • MATHEMATICS

Building
For Earthquakes

Grades 6–8

Glenview, Illinois • Boston, Massachusetts • Chandler, Arizona • Upper Saddle River, New Jersey

Teacher Reviewers

Candida M. Braun
West Fargo Public Schools
West Fargo, North Dakota

Sherri M. Gibson
Union Elementary STEM and
Demonstration School
Gallatin, Tennessee

Susan Holt
Union Elementary STEM and
Demonstration School
Gallatin, Tennessee

L. Jean Jackson
Old Mill Middle South
Annapolis, Maryland

Paul Keidel
Bismarck Public Schools
Bismarck, North Dakota

Martin Laine
Ayer-Shirley Middle School
Ayer, Massachusetts

Angelia Joy Long
Charles Carroll Middle School
New Carrollton, Maryland

Linda McShane
La Grange Public Schools District 102
La Grange Park, Illinois

Diana Mitchell
Union Elementary STEM and
Demonstration School
Gallatin, Tennessee

Bradd Smithson
John Glenn Middle School
Bedford, Massachusetts

Mary Reid Thompson
Union Elementary STEM and
Demonstration School
Gallatin, Tennessee

Leslie Yates
Union Elementary STEM and
Demonstration School
Gallatin, Tennessee

Acknowledgments

Photographs

Every effort has been made to secure permission and provide appropriate credit for photographic material. The publisher deeply regrets any omission and pledges to correct errors called to its attention in subsequent editions.

Unless otherwise acknowledged, all photographs are the property of Pearson Education, Inc.

Photo locators denoted as follows: Top (T), Center (C), Bottom (B), Left (L), Right (R), Background (Bkgd)

Building for Earthquakes
Cover: (R) ©3DDock/Shutterstock, (CL) ©advent/Shutterstock, (BCL) ©Anatoly Vartanov/iStockphoto, (L) ©casejustin/Shutterstock, (C) ©Rudyanto Wijaya/iStockphoto; **ivE** Eckehard Schulz/©Associated Press; **vE** (CR) Car Culture/Corbis; **viiE** ©Kimimasa Mayama/Reuters/Landov LLC; **ixE** National Institute of Standards and Technology; **xE** ©2011, Texas A&M University.

Designing Space Vehicles
Cover: (L) ©1971yes/Shutterstock, (BR) ©BiterBig/Shutterstock, (CR) ©Rafael Pacheco/Shutterstock; **ivS** Eckehard Schulz/©Associated Press; **vS** (CR) Car Culture/Corbis; **viiiS** ©HO/EPN/NewsCom, ixS NASA, **xS** (L) ©Gabriel Bouys/AFP/Getty Images, **xS** (R) ©NJC-Kemsley/Mirrorpix/Newscom.

ISBN-13: 978-0-13-319674-0
ISBN-10: 0-13-319674-7
4 5 6 7 8 9 10   V011   15 14 13

Project STEM

Introduction to STEM

Building for Earthquakes

Appendices

Review the Safety Symbols pages before beginning each topic.

The Engineering Design Process

Engineers are people who use scientific and technological knowledge to solve practical problems. To design new products, engineers usually follow the process described here, even though they may not follow these steps in the same order each time.

Identify a Need

Before engineers begin designing a new product, they must first identify the need they are trying to meet or the problem they want to solve. For example, suppose you are a member of a design team in a company that makes model cars. Your team has identified a need: a model car that is inexpensive and easy to assemble.

Research the Problem

Engineers often begin by gathering information that will help them with their new design. This research may include finding articles in books, in journals, or on the Internet. It may also involve talking to other engineers who have solved similar problems. Engineers often perform experiments related to the product they want to design.

For your model car, you could look at cars that are similar to the one you want to design. You might do research on the Internet. You could also test some materials to see whether they will work well in a model car.

Design a Solution

Brainstorm Ideas When engineers design new products, they usually work in teams. Design teams often hold brainstorming meetings in which any team member can contribute ideas. Brainstorming is a creative process in which one team member's suggestions often spark ideas in other group members. Brainstorming can lead to new approaches to solving a design problem.

Document the Process As the design team works, its members document, or keep a record of, the process. Having access to documentation enables others to repeat, or replicate, the process in the future. Design teams document their research sources, ideas, lists of materials, and so on because any part of the process may be a helpful resource later.

Identify Constraints During brainstorming, a design team may come up with several possible designs. To better focus their ideas, team members consider constraints. A constraint is a factor that limits a product design. Physical characteristics, such as the properties of materials used to make your model car, are constraints. Money and time are also constraints. If the materials in a product cost a lot or if the product takes a long time to make, the design may be impractical.

Make Trade-offs Design teams usually need to make trade-offs. In a trade-off, engineers give up one benefit of a proposed design in order to obtain another. In designing your model car, you might have to make trade-offs. For example, you might decide to give up the benefit of sturdiness in order to obtain the benefit of lower cost.

ivE

Building for Earthquakes

Select a Solution After considering the constraints and trade-offs of the possible designs, engineers then select one idea to develop further. That idea represents the solution that the team thinks best meets the need or solves the problem that was identified at the beginning of the process. The decision includes selecting the materials that will be used in the first attempt to build a product.

Build, Test, and Evaluate a Prototype

Once the team has chosen a design plan, the engineers build a prototype. A prototype is a working model used to test a design. Engineers evaluate the prototype to see whether it meets the goal. They must determine whether it works well, is easy to operate, is safe to use, and holds up to repeated use.

Part of the evaluation includes collecting data in the form of measurements. For example, think of your model car. Once you decide how to build your prototype, what would you want to know about it? You might want to measure how much baggage it could carry or how its shape affects its speed.

Communicate the Solution

A team needs to communicate the final design to the people who will manufacture and use the product. To do this, teams may use sketches, detailed drawings, computer simulations, and written descriptions. The team may also present the evidence that was collected when the prototype was tested. This evidence may include mathematical representations, such as graphs and data tables, that support the choice for the final design.

Troubleshoot and Redesign

Few prototypes work perfectly, which is why they need to be tested. Once a design team has tested a prototype, the members analyze the results and identify any problems. The team then tries to troubleshoot, or fix, the design problems. Troubleshooting allows the team to redesign the prototype to improve on how well the solution meets the need.

Science, Technology, Engineering, and Math

In your school, you probably have separate math, science, social studies, and English classes. Does that mean that you'll never use English in your math class or knowledge of geography in your science class? No! It turns out that the knowledge and skills you learn in one class or subject area will help you in other areas as well. This is especially true in the areas of STEM: Science, Technology, Engineering, and Math.

Science tries to understand the natural world and discover new knowledge. Engineers then use that knowledge to create solutions to problems through the development or use of technologies. Technology, engineering, and even math all work with science to expand our knowledge of the world around us.

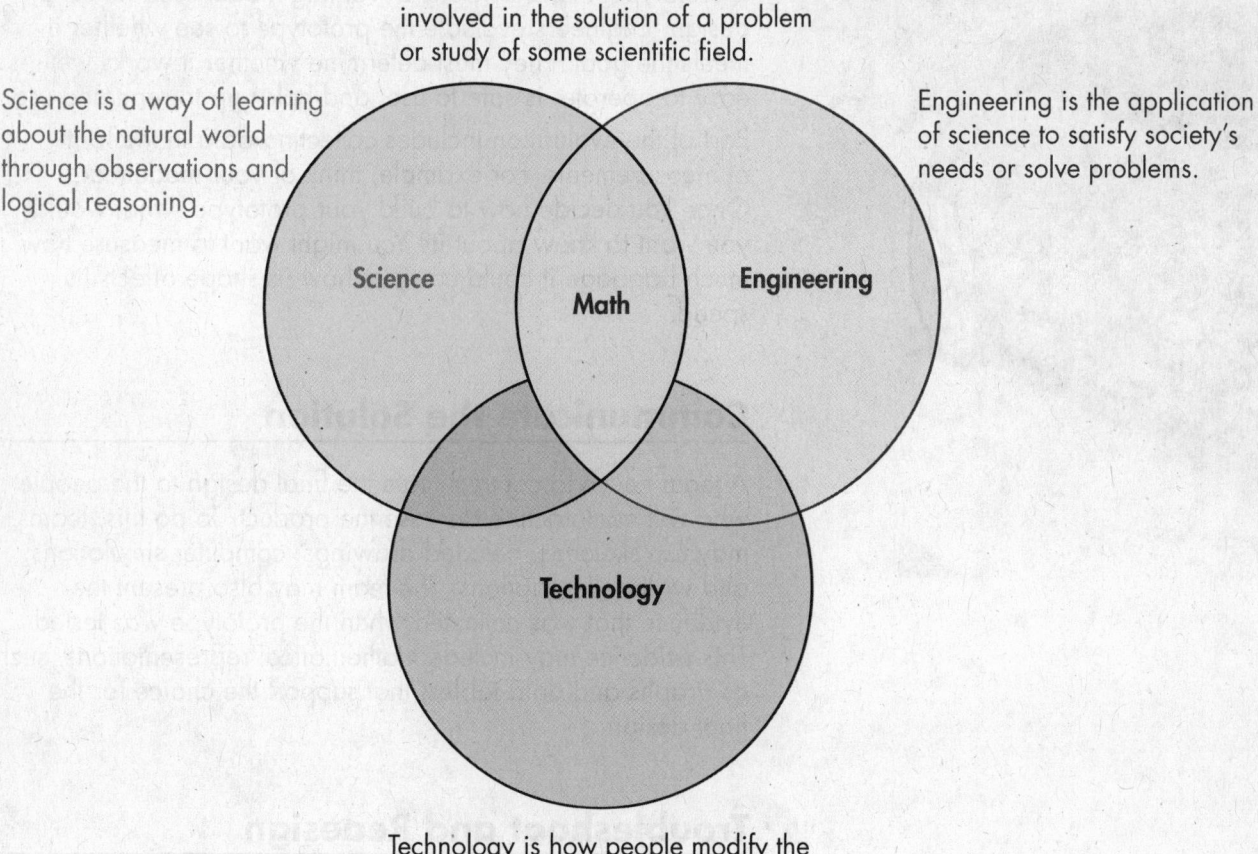

Math is the operations and processes involved in the solution of a problem or study of some scientific field.

Science is a way of learning about the natural world through observations and logical reasoning.

Engineering is the application of science to satisfy society's needs or solve problems.

Science

Math

Engineering

Technology

Technology is how people modify the world around them to meet their needs or to solve practical problems.

Scientific Inquiry Process and Engineering Design Process

Scientists and engineers use similar structured processes to do their work. These processes allow the scientists and engineers to work through questions or problems. Even if you're not a scientist or an engineer, these processes might help you answer a question or solve a problem!

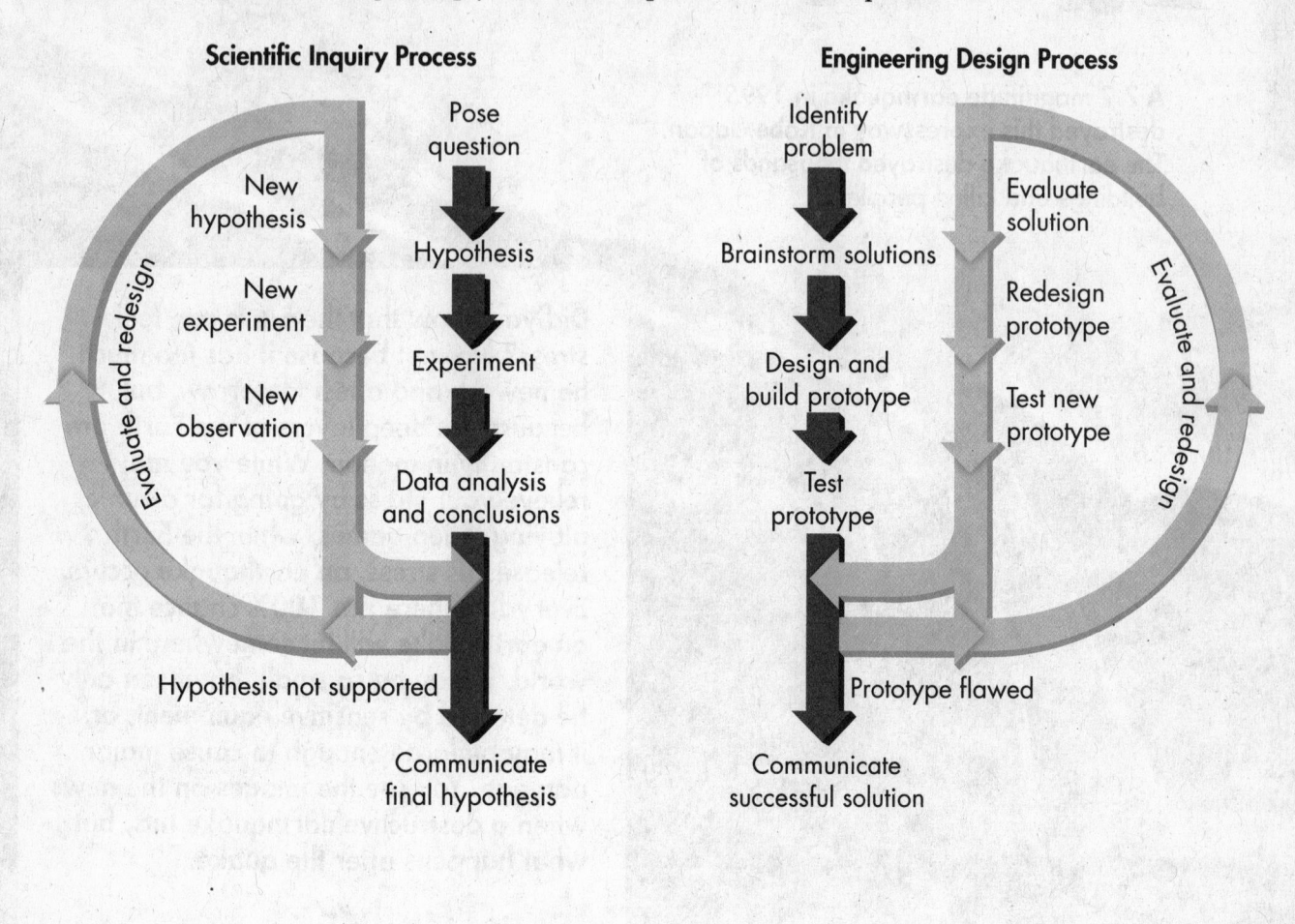

Scientific Inquiry Process

Pose question → Hypothesis → Experiment → Data analysis and conclusions

New hypothesis, New experiment, New observation

Evaluate and redesign

Hypothesis not supported

Communicate final hypothesis

Engineering Design Process

Identify problem → Brainstorm solutions → Design and build prototype → Test prototype

Evaluate solution, Redesign prototype, Test new prototype

Evaluate and redesign

Prototype flawed

Communicate successful solution

Introduction to
Earthquakes

A 7.2 magnitude earthquake in 1995 destroyed this expressway in Kobe, Japan. The earthquake destroyed thousands of buildings and killed people.

Did you know that the Earth can feel stress? No, not because it has too much homework and a test tomorrow, but because the deep layers of the Earth are constantly in motion. While you may relieve your stress by going for a run or playing video games, when the Earth releases its stress, an earthquake occurs. Everyday, there is a 100% chance that an earthquake will hit somewhere in the world. It may be so small that it can only be detected by sensitive equipment, or it may be large enough to cause major damage. You see the images on the news when a destructive earthquake hits, but what happens after the quake.

Take It Further

Go to the U.S. Geological Survey website at www.usgs.gov and click on Real-Time Earthquakes: Worldwide and the United States. Using these maps, find the number of earthquakes that have occurred in your community. Then identify which areas in the world had the most activity. Compare your location to these areas and explain why you think certain areas had more activity.

Rescue Robots

An earthquake hits every day somewhere in the world, but scientists are unable to predict when or where one will strike. Nor can they predict the strength of the quake and the damage it will cause. So, scientists, roboticists, and engineers focus on what to do after an earthquake. Roboticists use math, science, and engineering to develop and perfect various types of robots. Rescue robots can enter areas devastated by earthquakes. These areas are often too dangerous for humans or rescue dogs to enter. They are unstable and may be polluted with chemicals or radiation. Robots that slither, slide, or crawl into the rubble can help rescue teams assess damage from afar. These robots can locate survivors, using heat and color sensing technology. They gather information about the area. The first use of robot rescuers in the U.S. came after the tragedy of 9/11. A group of roboticists, led by Dr. Robin Murphy, was invited to New York after the disaster. Today, Dr. Murphy runs "Roboticists Without Borders" at Texas A&M University. Together with other groups, Roboticists Without Borders sends robots to aid rescue efforts worldwide.

Take It Further

Rescue robots have been used following major disasters, such as 9/11, Hurricane Katrina, and the 2011 earthquake in Japan. Use the Internet to research universities, such as Texas A&M, government agencies, and companies that are developing and testing rescue robots. Find out what skills and education are needed for a career in robotics. Then use this information to write a job advertisement seeking a roboticist.

After an earthquake, rescue robots can move through the rubble that would be unsafe for people or animals. Robots can get into tiny spaces and search for survivors or send information about the damage to rescuers.

ixE

Robots with Personality

Imagine you have just survived an earthquake and are trapped beneath a pile of rubble. It is dark, the air is filled with dust, and you can't hear anything from the outside world. Suddenly bright lights blind you and a black robot approaches you. Its voice is loud and it invades your personal space. You don't know how to respond to this creepy figure. How do you think you would feel? Scared? Angry? Frustrated? These are the emotions roboticists at Texas A&M's Center for Robot-Assisted Search and Rescue want to ease. For victims of disasters, a rescue robot may be the only link to the outside world. To take the "creepy" out of rescue robots, roboticists are working to create a friendlier version of the rescue robot called the "Survivor Buddy." An animator from Pixar® is helping to design movements that will

be more calming to survivors. Two-way video and Web-streaming will help reduce anxiety and aid in rescue efforts. This new technology is designed to help victims remain calm, allowing human rescuers to better do their jobs.

Take It Further

Research photos online of different rescue robots, such as the Urban Search and Rescue Robot (USAR). For ideas, you may also want to research Pixar to see some of their "human-like" animated objects. Then, working with a team, give the rescue robot you choose a personality makeover. Think about colors and human attributes that are calming, such as a pleasant voice or a friendly smile. The goal of your design is to get the "creepy" out of a rescue robot.

The Survivor Buddy allows survivors trapped beneath rubble to communicate with rescue workers on the ground. It can also stream radio and television to help victims remain calm. Dr. Murphy worked with sociologists to give Survivor Buddy behaviors that will be sympathetic and human-like.

xE

Quick Lab
How Do Seismic Waves Travel Through Earth?

An earthquake results from the movement of rock beneath Earth's surface and releases tremendous amounts of stored energy. Some of this energy travels as seismic waves through Earth's interior and across its surface.

Inquiry Focus Observe

Materials Spring toy

Procedure

1. With a partner, experiment with the spring toy to see how many different types of wave motions you can produce. Stretch the spring toy across the floor while your partner holds the other end. Do not overstretch. Then try making wave motions.

2. Gather together about four coils of the spring toy, and then release them at the same time. Observe the direction in which the coils move.

3. Once the coils have stopped moving, jerk one end of the toy from side to side once. Be sure your partner has a secure grip on the other end. Observe the direction in which the coils move.

Think It Over

4. Describe the wave motions you observed in Steps 2 and 3.

_____

_____

_____

_____

_____

5. Predict what the two different waves might feel like if you were standing on Earth's surface above them.

_____

_____

_____

_____

_____

_____

_____

Vocabulary Practice

Use your textbook or a dictionary to define the science, technology, engineering, and math terms in the chart below. Complete the chart by writing a strategy to help you remember the meaning of each term. One has been done for you.

Term	Definition	How I'm going to remember the meaning
stress	a force that acts on a rock to change its shape or volume	When I squeeze a water balloon and it changes shape, I have applied a stress.
tension		
fault		
focus		
epicenter		
seismic wave		
magnitude		
seismograph		
engineer		
ratio		

2E

Building for Earthquakes

Ratios and Proportions Making a Scale Diagram

A scale is the ratio of the measurements in a drawing to the actual measurements of the objects drawn. A scale diagram is a drawing made so that distances in the drawing are proportional to actual distances.

> **HOW** You Will Use this **Skill in Science**
> ....
> • Mapping Earth
> • Reading Maps
> • Building Models
> • Drawing Diagrams

Example 1 Use the scale diagram below to find the actual length of the room.

Step 1 Measure the length in centimeters. The room is 5 cm long in the diagram.

Step 2 Write the ratio of the length in the drawing to the actual length ℓ.

$$\frac{5 \text{ cm}}{\ell \text{ m}}$$

Step 3 Write a proportion relating the ratio to the scale. Then solve for ℓ.

$$\frac{5 \text{ cm}}{\ell \text{ m}} = \frac{1 \text{ cm}}{1 \text{ m}}$$

$\ell = 5$ m, so the actual length of the room is 5 m.

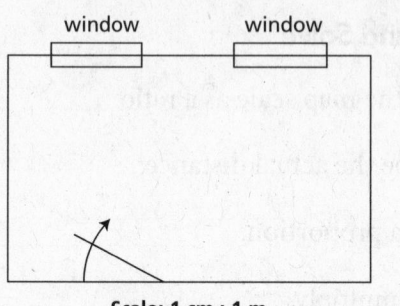

Scale: 1 cm : 1 m

Example 2 A scale in a diagram is 4 cm : 10 m. If the distance in the diagram is 9 cm, find the actual distance.

Step 1 Write a proportion. Let the actual distance be d.

$$\frac{10 \text{ m}}{4 \text{ cm}} = \frac{d \text{ m}}{9 \text{ cm}}$$

Step 2 Cross-multiply. Cancel units.

$$10 \text{ m} \times 9 \text{ cm} = 4 \text{ cm} \times d \text{ m}$$

$$\frac{10 \text{ m} \times 9 \text{ cm}}{4 \text{ cm}} = d \text{ m} \qquad \text{So, } d = 22.5 \text{ m.}$$

TRY IT YOURSELF!

Use a centimeter ruler and the scale diagram above.

1. Find the width of the room.

2. Find the distance between the windows.

3. A scale diagram of a building is 2 cm : 10 m. If the length in the diagram is 3.5 cm, what is the actual length of the building?

Ratios and Proportions Mapping Earth

A map scale is a ratio that compares a distance on the map to the actual distance on Earth's surface. For example, 1 cm : 10 km means that 1 cm on the map equals 10 km on the ground. You can also use actual distances to make a map scale.

Sample Problem: The scale on a highway map is 2 cm : 5 km. The distance between two cities is 17 cm on the map. What is the actual distance between the cities?

1. Read and Understand

What information is given? (the map scale, 2 cm : 5 km, and the distance between the cities on the map, 17 cm)

What are you asked to find? (the actual distance in kilometers between the cities)

2. Plan and Solve

Write the map scale as a ratio. $\dfrac{5 \text{ km}}{2 \text{ cm}}$

Let d be the actual distance.

Write a proportion. $\dfrac{d \text{ km}}{17 \text{ cm}} = \dfrac{5 \text{ km}}{2 \text{ cm}}$

Cross-multiply. $d \text{ km} \times 2 \text{ cm} = 5 \text{ km} \times 17 \text{ cm}$

Solve for d. Cancel units. $d \text{ km} = \dfrac{5 \text{ km} \times 17 \text{ cm}}{2 \text{ cm}}$

$d = 42.5 \text{ km}$

So, the actual distance between the two cities is 43 km.

3. Look Back and Check

Is the answer reasonable? (Yes; substituting $d = 42.5$ km into the proportion makes the cross-products equal. The actual distance is rounded to 2 significant figures.)

TRY IT YOURSELF!

1. The scale on a trail map is 0.5 cm : 1 km. The straight distance between 2 huts on the trail is 16.9 cm. What is the actual distance?

2. The scale on an aerial photograph is 1 cm : 2.5 km. The length of a lake is 2.7 cm on the photograph. What is the actual length of the lake?

3. The scale on a highway map is 5 cm : 50 km. Suppose you know that the actual distance between two towns is 240 km. On the map, the distance is 12 cm. Is the scale on the map correct? Explain.

4. Suppose you are making a map of a square area. The dimensions of the actual area are 1,000 km by 1,000 km. You are drawing the map on a grid that is 10 cm by 10 cm. What scale would you use? Two cities are 820 km apart on the ground. How far apart are they on your map?

Building for Earthquakes

Technology Zone How Do Seismographs Work?

You have probably seen zigzag lines, like the ones shown below, used to represent an earthquake. The pattern of lines, called a seismogram, is the record of an earthquake's seismic waves. It is produced by an instrument called a seismograph.

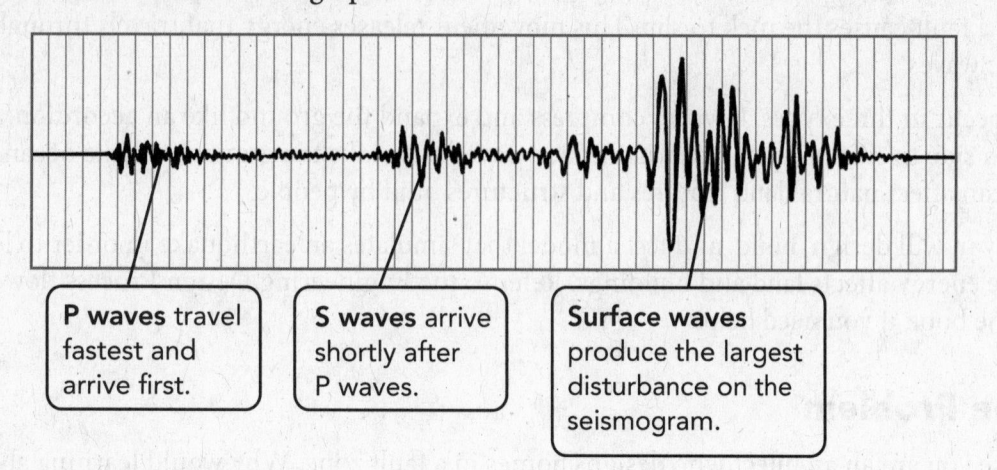

P waves travel fastest and arrive first.

S waves arrive shortly after P waves.

Surface waves produce the largest disturbance on the seismogram.

Measuring Seismic Waves When you write a sentence, the paper stays in one place while your hand moves the pen. But in a seismograph, the pen remains stationary while the paper moves.

A simple seismograph can consist of a heavy weight attached to a frame by a spring or wire. A pen connected to the weight rests its point on a drum that can rotate. The height of the lines drawn by the seismograph is greater for a more severe earthquake or an earthquake closer to the seismograph.

Modern seismographs are complex electronic devices. In addition to the severity of the shaking, they also record the precise timing of the shaking. Some laptop computers and car air bags contain similar devices that detect shaking.

Design It

Car air bags use a device that is similar to a seismograph. Work with a partner to answer the following questions.

1. Why do you think car designers included such an instrument? Explain your thinking.

   _____

   _____

2. Name at least two reasons for including a seismograph-like device in an automobile.

   _____

   _____

3. What other industries do you think might use motion detectors similar to a seismograph?

   _____

   _____

Building for Earthquakes

STEM Project Shake, Rattle, and Roll

Earth's surface is made up of rigid tectonic plates that rest and gradually move atop its elastic mantle. Forces from tectonic plate movement cause stress on the brittle crust at Earth's surface. When enough stress builds up, the rocky crust breaks, forming a fault. An earthquake occurs when the stress along a fault causes the rock to slip. This movement releases energy that travels through Earth as seismic waves.

Seismic waves occur in three types. P waves compress and expand the ground like an accordion. S waves can vibrate from side to side or up and down. Surface waves can make the ground roll like ocean waves. Seismic waves can affect natural land features and structures built by people.

In this activity, you will design, build, and test a model that simulates an earthquake in order to learn how earthquake energy affects land and buildings. Refer to the Engineering Design Process flowchart in the middle of the book if you need help.

Identify the Problem

☑ **1.** Suppose you are an architect who designs homes in a fault zone. Why would learning about earthquakes be important to you?

_____

_____

_____

Do Research

Examine the diagrams of faults and seismic waves.

☑ **2.** What physical features should be visible in an earthquake model?

_____

_____

_____

_____

☑ **3.** Which aspects of an earthquake are important to demonstrate in a working model? Explain.

_____

_____

_____

_____

_____

Building for Earthquakes

Go to the materials station(s). Examine the materials. Think about which materials may be useful for your model. Leave the materials where they are.

☑ **4.** What are your design constraints?

_____

_____

_____

_____

Develop Possible Solutions

☑ **5.** Describe ways in which you could use the materials to build a model of Earth's surface at a fault. Identify at least two ways you could simulate earthquake motion in your model.

_____

_____

_____

_____

Choose One Solution

Write your answers to Questions 6–8 on the next page.

☑ **6.** List the material(s) you will use for your earthquake model.

☑ **7.** Draw your design and label all the parts. Describe how you will build your earthquake model.

☑ **8.** Describe how your model will simulate the motion of an earthquake.

Building for Earthquakes

☐ = 1 cm

Ideas, Drawings, and Answers

Design and Construct a Prototype

Have your teacher review and approve your design. Then gather the materials you need to build your earthquake model. The structure you build will be your prototype, the first working version of your design. If you can, document your construction process by taking photos or recording video as you go. Be sure to wear goggles as you build and then test your prototype.

☑ **9.** Measure the dimensions of your prototype. Record the design details.

_____

_____

_____

☑ **10.** On the next page, draw a detailed diagram of your prototype. Label the features and measurements.

Test the Prototype

Test your prototype. Use whatever method you have developed to simulate the motion of an earthquake. Observe what effects the motion has on the land features and the built structures you included in your prototype.

☑ **11.** Circle the wave motions your prototype simulated.

P wave motion   S wave motion   surface wave motion

☑ **12.** How did your simulated earthquake motion affect the land and buildings in your prototype?

_____

_____

_____

☑ **13.** On the next page, draw in detail what your prototype looks like after the test.

Building for Earthquakes

Name _____ Date _____ Class _____

Ideas, Drawings, and Answers

☐ = 1 cm

10E

Building for Earthquakes

Communicate Results

☑ **14.** Collect the materials that document the design, construction, and testing of your prototype. Assemble a portfolio that includes the before and after diagrams of the land area, your photographs of the process, and a record of your test results. Prepare a data table to display information about the duration and type of movement and the results in your prototype. Write a short summary of how data like yours could be useful to an architect trying to design safer homes.

☑ **15.** Prepare a computer slide show or a video presentation showing how you built your prototype, how it performed, and why your results were significant. Include your conclusions on how the earthquake motion would affect natural features and built structures near the fault. Deliver the presentation to your class.

Evaluate and Redesign

☑ **16.** Evaluate your prototype using the following rubric. Check one answer for each question.

Does the prototype...	Very Much	Somewhat	Not at All
fit onto the provided base?			
include a representation of a fault?			
represent natural land features?			
represent built structures?			
show the effects of the earthquake motion?			

☑ **17.** Compare your results with those of your classmates. Did your prototypes function in similar ways? Explain.

_____

_____

_____

_____

☑ **18.** What changes could you make to your earthquake prototype to make it a more accurate representation of how earthquakes affect land and buildings?

_____

_____

_____

_____

Building for Earthquakes

Name _____   Date _____   Class _____

Ideas, Drawings, and Answers

☐ = 1 cm

Career Spotlight Structural Engineer

Civil engineers design things in your community such as roads, water treatment facilities, buildings, airports, and train stations.

A structural engineer is a civil engineer who specializes in the design of safe structures. Structural engineers design bridges, tunnels, and freeway interchanges. They need to design safe structures that can withstand forces such as gravity, wind, soil movement, and earthquakes.

Since structures are built on soil, the design of a building also requires knowledge of the soil it is built on. If the soil is unstable, the foundation needs to be designed to create stability, and the soil may need to be compacted, excavated, or reinforced before construction begins. If a structure is located in an earthquake zone, the building and its foundation need to be built to withstand the shaking motion of an earthquake.

Structural engineers often work in teams to design a structure and create plans and drawings for all the necessary components. Plans include scale drawings and measurements for all structural components.

Design It

Quick Activity A

Work with a partner. You will need a stack of cards and a sheet of paper. Using the stack of cards, you will construct a house of cards that can withstand earthquake-like conditions. You must build your house on the sheet of paper. Before you begin construction, discuss design constraints with your partner. You have 10 minutes to build your house.

After 10 minutes, one of you will slide or shake the paper to simulate an earthquake. Did your house survive? Which parts? _____

_____

Quick Activity B

You will redesign your house of cards using toothpicks as supports. Discuss with your partner how the toothpicks will make the house of cards more stable. Where should the toothpicks be placed for greatest structural support? _____

Now draw a diagram of a house of cards with the additional support.

Name _____ Date _____ Class _____

Hands-on Inquiry Finding the Epicenter

Reviewing Content

An earthquake occurs when rock that is under stress below Earth's surface breaks and releases energy. The *focus* is the place underground where the rock breaks. Seismic waves move out from the focus in all directions, carrying energy.

The epicenter is the point on Earth's surface directly above the focus. The strength of an earthquake is greatest at its epicenter, and this is typically where the most damage occurs.

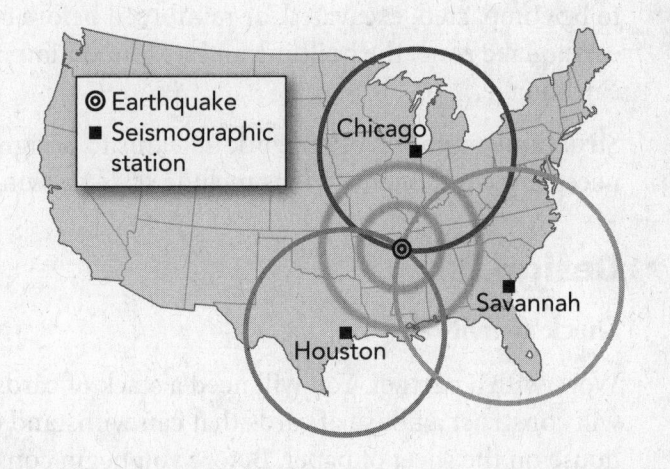

Scientists can use data from seismographs to determine the location of the epicenter. A seismograph records both P and S waves as they arrive at the seismograph location. Although P and S waves start out at exactly the same time when an earthquake occurs, P waves travel faster and reach the seismograph first. S waves arrive second. Scientists can use these data (recorded on a seismogram) to measure the difference in arrival time between P and S waves. The farther apart the arrival times of the waves are, the farther the location is from the epicenter.

Reviewing Inquiry Focus

Scientists interpret data so they can draw conclusions about their hypotheses. Interpreting data means making sense out of the data gathered during an experiment by looking at patterns or trends. Data can be displayed in different ways. A data table is an organized way to record observations from an experiment. A graph is another way to organize data. Graphs can be better than data tables for showing patterns and trends in the data.

1. In this Lab Investigation, what data are you given to analyze? In what formats are the data presented?

   _____

   _____

2. What conclusion will you be able to draw after analyzing the data?

   _____

   _____

   _____

   _____

Hands-on Inquiry Finding the Epicenter

You will need to refer to this graph as you conduct your experiment. The graph shows how the difference in arrival time between P waves and S waves is related to the distance from the epicenter of the earthquake.

Find the difference in arrival time for Denver on the *y*-axis of the graph. Follow this line across to the point at which it crosses the curve. To find the distance to the epicenter, read down from this point to the *x*-axis of the graph.

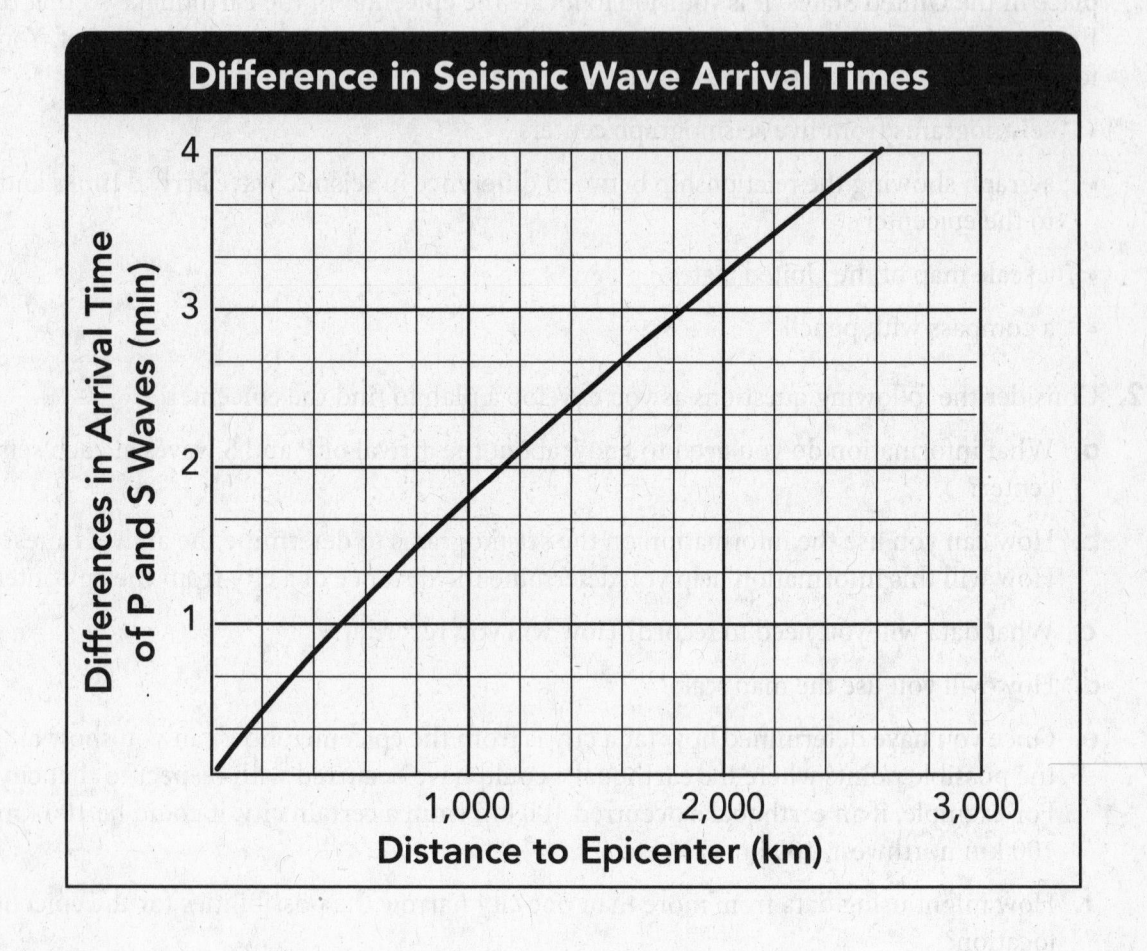

Difference in Seismic Wave Arrival Times

Differences in Arrival Time of P and S Waves (min)

Distance to Epicenter (km)

Hands-on Inquiry Finding the Epicenter

Problem How can you locate an earthquake's epicenter?

Inquiry Focus Interpret Data • Draw Conclusions

Design an Experiment

1. Suppose you are a seismologist and have just found out about a major earthquake that has taken place in the United States. It is your job to locate the epicenter of the earthquake so that the Federal Emergency Management Agency (FEMA) will know where to focus its disaster relief. You have the following information and tools available:

   - seismograms from five seismograph centers

   - a graph showing the relationship between difference in seismic wave arrival times and distance to the epicenter

   - a scale map of the United States

   - a compass with pencil

2. Consider the following questions as you develop a plan to find the epicenter:

   a. What information do you need to know about the arrival of P and S waves at each seismograph center?

   b. How can you use the information on the seismograms to determine the arrival times? How will this information help you determine the distance of a city from the epicenter?

   c. What data will you need to record? How will you record it?

   d. How will you use the map scale?

   e. Once you have determined how far a city is from the epicenter, how can you show all the possible points where the earthquake could have occurred with respect to that city? For example, if an earthquake occurred 100 km from a certain city, it could be 100 km north, 100 km northwest, 100 km east, etc.

   f. How might using data from more than one city narrow the possibilities for the epicenter location?

Name _____ Date _____ Class _____

3. Write out your step-by-step procedure for finding the epicenter. Draw any data tables you will need. Have your teacher approve your plan.

4. Carry out your procedure and record your data. If you need additional space, use the next page.

Procedure

_____

_____

_____

_____

Data Table

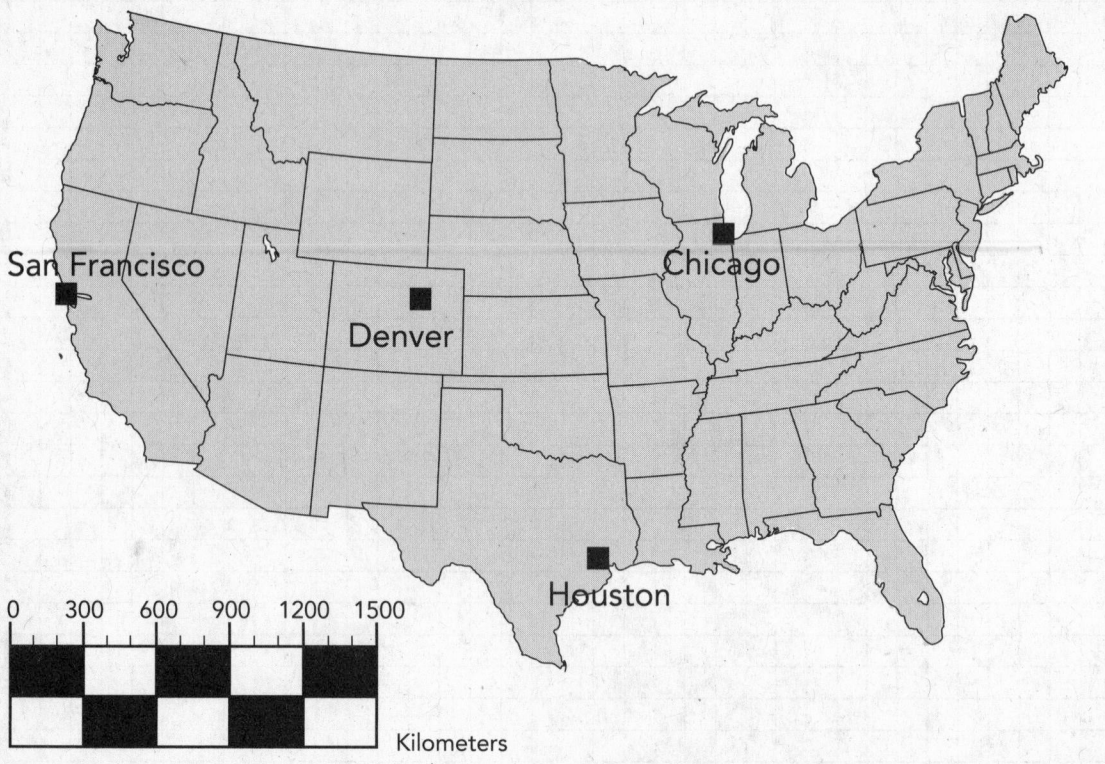

Building for Earthquakes

Ideas, Drawings, and Answers

☐ = 1 cm

Analyze and Conclude

5. Interpret Data Look at the circles you have drawn on the map. There should be various points of intersection. What do these points represent?

_____

_____

_____

6. Observe Where is the epicenter of the earthquake?

_____

_____

_____

7. Calculate Mark a point on the map that is 2,400 km from the epicenter, in any direction you wish. What would you expect the difference in arrival time between P and S waves to be at this point?

_____

_____

_____

8. Draw Conclusions Suppose that the three circles you draw to determine an epicenter do not intersect exactly at one point. The diagram on the right shows this type of situation. Suggest a strategy for determining the epicenter.

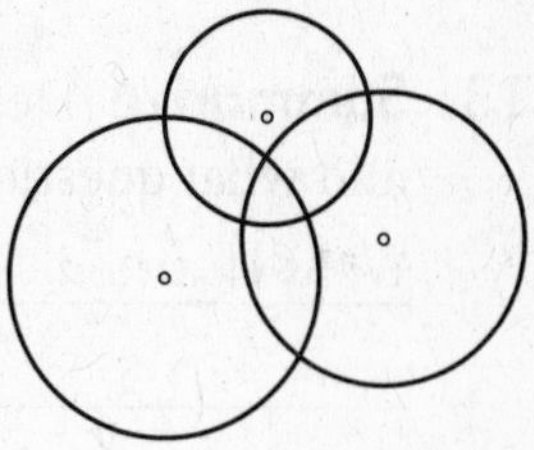

_____

_____

_____

_____

9. Develop a Hypothesis Imagine you are given a new set of seismograms from five different locations. You follow the same procedure you carried out in this Lab Investigation to determine the location of the epicenter. However, as you draw circles with your compass, you find that one circle does not intersect any of the others. Develop a hypothesis to explain this outlying circle.

_____

_____

_____

_____

_____

Building for Earthquakes

POST LAB

Hands-on Inquiry Finding the Epicenter

10. Design an Experiment What sources of error might be encountered in this activity that could affect the results?

_____

_____

11. Predict Suppose an earthquake struck California, and its epicenter was 100 km north of San Francisco. Predict three pieces of data you could obtain from the P and S waves from this earthquake.

_____

_____

12. Observe Imagine you have two seismograms from different cities. How could you determine which city is closer to the epicenter simply by looking at the seismograms?

_____

_____

13. Summarize Describe what you learned in this lab about finding the epicenter of an earthquake and what questions you still have.

What I learned _____

_____

_____

What I still want to know _____

_____

_____

Communicate

Relate Evidence and Explanation Join forces with another lab group. Your task is to create a short television news report that explains how you determined the epicenter of the earthquake. Your news report should include

- an explanation of a seismograph and what it detects;
- an explanation of P and S waves;
- an explanation of the procedure you took in this lab to determine the epicenter;
- the use of specific examples in your explanations.

Ideas, Drawings, and Answers

☐ = 1 cm

21E

Building for Earthquakes

Name _____ Date _____ Class _____

Enrichment Monitoring Earthquakes

Read the passage and look at the diagram. Then answer the questions.

Earthquake Probability

This combined map and bar graph shows the probability of earthquakes in different areas along the San Andreas Fault. Probability is a measure of how likely it is that some event will happen in a given time. A probability near 100 percent means that an event is very likely to happen. A probability near zero percent means that an event is very unlikely to happen.

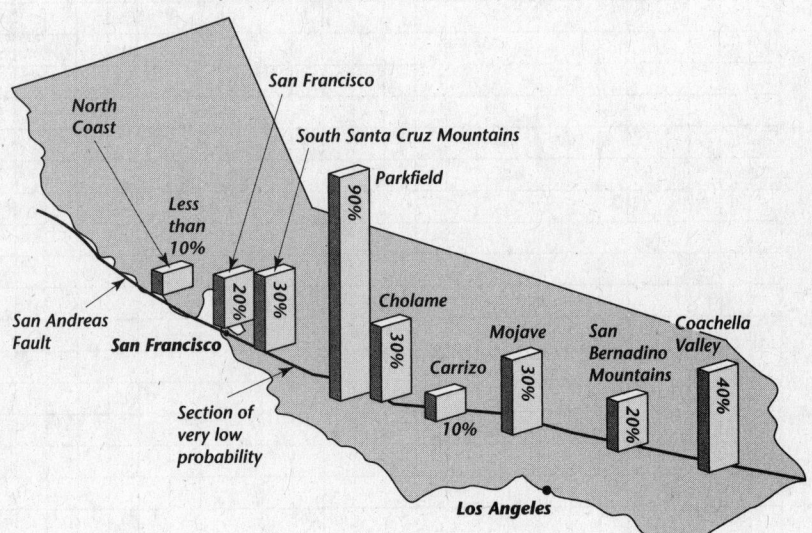

Earthquake Probability Along the San Andreas Fault

1. Which area has the highest probability of an earthquake?

    _____
    _____

2. What is the probability of an earthquake in the North Coast area?

    _____
    _____

3. The fault section between the South Santa Cruz Mountains and Parkfield has a very low probability. Geologists know that this area has experienced very little damaging seismic activity in the past. They also found that the blocks of rock in this section move slowly and continually. Why would slow, continual movement lead geologists to give the section a low probability?

    _____
    _____
    _____
    _____

4. What can you infer about why the probability of an earthquake is so high in the Parkfield area?

    _____
    _____
    _____
    _____

Building for Earthquakes

Assessment Earthquakes and Seismic Waves

If the statement is true, write *true*. If the statement is false, change the underlined word or words to make the statement true.

1. _____ The shaking and trembling that results from movement of <u>rock</u> beneath Earth's surface is called an earthquake.

2. _____ On a seismogram, higher lines drawn on the paper indicate <u>weaker</u> seismic waves.

3. _____ <u>P waves</u> can become surface waves when they reach Earth's surface.

Fill in the blank to complete each statement.

4. The _____ of an earthquake is the point where rock under stress begins to break or move.

5. The weight and pen of a seismograph resist _____ during an earthquake.

6. A _____ engineer specializes in the design of safe structures.

7. You want to make a scale model of a sailboat that is 16 m long and 15 m tall. You plan to make the model 43 cm long. What will be the height of the model?_____

APPLY THE BIG ❓ How are buildings designed to withstand earthquakes?

8. An architect is hired to design a skyscraper in the Indonesian city of Jakarta, which is near the Ring of Fire, an active earthquake and volcano zone. The architect must follow special building codes that the city has written. What might those codes be for, and why are they important in Jakarta?

_____

_____

_____

_____

_____

_____

_____

_____

_____

Performance Assessment Seismic-Safe Buildings

Suppose you are on the highest floor of a tall building in your town. An earthquake strikes. What features might help the building withstand the powerful effects of an earthquake? Civil engineers use different technologies to design buildings that can withstand earthquakes.

Seismic-safe buildings have features that reduce earthquake damage. Some of these features strengthen a building. Others allow the building to move or shield the building from the energy of seismic waves. In earthquake-prone areas, most tall steel-frame buildings may have one or more of the seismic-safe features described here.

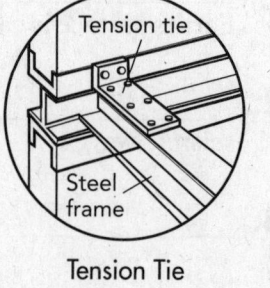

Tension Tie

To prevent cracks, tension ties are used to firmly "tie" the floors and ceilings of the building to the walls. Tension ties absorb and scatter earthquake energy and thus reduce damage.

Base isolation is another technology. In this type of design, the building is built on rubber pads or rollers. These structures separate, or isolate, the building from its foundation. The pads, like the ones shown to the right, stop some of an earthquake's energy from entering the building. When the earth shakes, the rollers allow the building to glide on top.

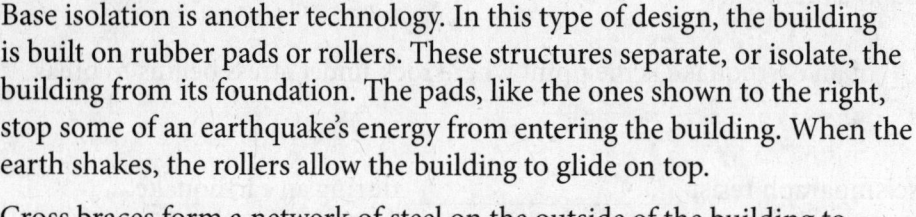

Base Isolator

Cross braces form a network of steel on the outside of the building to stiffen its frame. They also absorb energy during an earthquake. Dampers are heavy weights placed on certain floors of a high-rise building. Dampers work like shock absorbers in a car, absorbing some of the energy of seismic waves.

Design It

1. **Modeling Seismic-Safe Design** Use cardboard, craft sticks, modeling clay, and other common materials to build a small-scale prototype of a seismic-safe building. Use at least two features described above. Review the Engineering Design Process if you need help.

2. **Scale Drawings** On the next page, make a scale drawing of your building prototype with labels showing the seismic features. Decide on a scale for your drawing. (For example, you might decide that 2 cm in your prototype will be represented by 1 cm in your drawing, so your drawing will be half as wide, long, and tall as your actual prototype. Your scale will be 2 cm : 1 cm.) Use a ruler to make your drawing neat and accurate, and write the scale at the bottom of your drawing.

3. **Testing** Place your building prototype on a table and drop a heavy book next to it. Then try bumping the table to shake the prototype sideways in different directions. How well does your prototype stand up? What changes could you make to improve your structure's stability?

_____

_____

Building for Earthquakes

Name _____ Date _____ Class _____

Ideas, Drawings, and Answers

☐ = 1 cm

Building for Earthquakes

Standardized Test Prep

Multiple Choice

Circle the letter of the best answer.

1. An earthquake occurs along a fault when

   A energy in the rock along the fault does not change for a long period of time.

   B stress in the rock along the fault causes the rock to melt.

   C enough energy builds up in the rock along the fault to cause the rock to break or slip.

   D energy in the rock along the fault is changed to heat.

2. How does the height of the lines drawn by a seismograph after a severe earthquake compare to those from a minor earthquake?

   A The lines are lower for a severe earthquake.

   B The lines are higher for a severe earthquake.

   C The lines for a severe earthquake and a minor earthquake are equal.

   D No lines are drawn for a minor earthquake.

3. When an earthquake occurs, seismic waves travel

   A only through the hanging wall.

   B only through the footwall.

   C outward from the focus.

   D inward to the epicenter.

4. Engineers have designed a new car. Which of the following trade-offs would have a negative impact on public safety?

   A choosing low-cost materials over good results in crash tests

   B choosing appearance over good results in crash tests

   C choosing a better music system over a better air-conditioning system

   D choosing a more powerful engine over better gas mileage

Constructed Response

Use the diagram to the right and your knowledge of science to help you answer Question 5. Write your answer below.

5. Explain how scientists use seismographic stations to determine the location of an earthquake's epicenter.

   _____

   _____

   _____

   _____

   _____

   _____

   _____

   _____

   _____

   _____

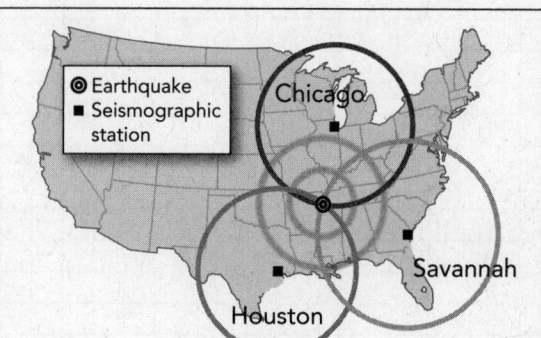

STEM Glossary